If you wanted to, and if you had the time to learn the necessary skills, do you believe that you could:

	Yes	No	Maybe
● Become an aircraft pilot or astronaut?	☐	☐	☐
● Write songs that get into the Top Ten?	☐	☐	☐
● Write good computer software programs?	☐	☐	☐
● Become a loving, caring parent?	☐	☐	☐
● Write a book?	☐	☐	☐
● Climb Mount Everest?	☐	☐	☐
● Run your own business?	☐	☐	☐
● Compete in the Olympics?	☐	☐	☐
● Become a doctor or a surgeon?	☐	☐	☐
● Become a Member of Parliament?	☐	☐	☐
● Hitchhike around the world?	☐	☐	☐
● Skydive?	☐	☐	☐
● Walk on fire?	☐	☐	☐
● Learn five foreign languages?	☐	☐	☐
● Become a disc jockey, singer or actor?	☐	☐	☐
● Become close friends with your own parents (as an equal person)?	☐	☐	☐
● Have a really happy, fulfilling marriage?	☐	☐	☐
● Organise something like Sport-Aid?	☐	☐	☐
● Run a marathon?	☐	☐	☐
● Bend metal just by looking at it?	☐	☐	☐
● Swim across the Channel?	☐	☐	☐
● Take stunning photographs?	☐	☐	☐
● Raise £10,000 for some special charity?	☐	☐	☐
● Be a manager of a modern factory?	☐	☐	☐
● Join Greenpeace on one of their missions?	☐	☐	☐
●	☐	☐	☐
●	☐	☐	☐

Five stateme

1 'You are full of i
you may not yet k

Do you believe th

2 'There are five b........
on the earth. You are a unique person. There is no one else like you on the whole earth.'

Do you believe this? Yes ☐ No ☐ Maybe ☐

3 'All humans are very special people, full of amazing abilities.'

Do you believe this? Yes ☐ No ☐ Maybe ☐

4 'There is nothing that you cannot do, if you really put your mind to it.'

Do you believe this? Yes ☐ No ☐ Maybe ☐

5 'If we wanted to and believed that it was possible, humans could end all war and hunger on the earth.'

Do you believe this? Yes ☐ No ☐ Maybe ☐

Whether you know it or not,
each of us is gifted,
each of us lives with a dream within,
each of us wants to be happy,
each of us wants to be successful, in our
  own way,
each of us wants to be loved by others,
each of us wants to have others to love,
each of us wants the world to be free of
  hunger and war,
each of us, deep down, wants to be loved
  by our parents,
each of us carries hurts and pains,
each of us carries fears and uncertainties,
each of us is trying to puzzle out what life
  is all about,
each of us is doing our best, in our own way,
and each of us is a child of nature,
a child of the universe.
Like arrows, coming from the past,
we reach into the unknown future.

For **you**, are these words:

. . . Basically true?   . . . Wishful thinking?
. . . Or just stupid?

3

How do you see yourself?

☐ I am a young person

☐ I am ———————————— (your name)

☐ I am hoping to find out who I am

☐ I am my parents' child

☐ I am a very special, gifted person

☐ I am what I am

☐ I am nobody special

☐ I am confused

☐ I am a mistake, and just a lot of trouble

☐ I am a citizen of Britain

☐ I am a citizen of the earth

☐ I am a child of the universe

☐ I am

☐

Use the blank spaces to describe who you are, and how you see yourself. Tick where you feel 'yes' to a statement.

Do you ever think about this kind of thing?

Yes ☐ No ☐ Sometimes ☐

Are you able to discuss this kind of thing with your friends?

Yes ☐ No ☐ Sometimes ☐

Are you happy to have been born on planet earth?

Yes ☐ No ☐ Sometimes ☐

Haven't decided yet ☐

Do you enjoy life?

1 You are sitting at home on your own.
A friend phones you up and invites you to go hang-gliding this weekend. You've never done it before. Do you accept?
(a) Yes (b) You say you'll come, but only to watch (c) No

2 Three other friends invite you to join them at a mixed-sex health club where there is a sauna and gym. Do you accept?
(a) Yes (b) You say you'll come if you can find a friend to go with (c) No

3 In two weeks' time, it will be your birthday, and also the birthday of two friends. How are you going to celebrate?
(a) By throwing a party (b) By agreeing to go out for a drink together (c) You'd prefer not to celebrate

4 You are invited on a two-week sailing holiday. You can swim, but you've never sailed before, and you have to find £50. Do you go for it?
(a) Yes (b) Yes, if someone gives me the money (c) No, I can't afford it

5 You are invited to join a sponsored walk over ten miles, to raise funds to fight famine. Do you join?
(a) Yes (b) Yes, if the weather is good and I feel up to it (c) No

6 A youth group from China is visiting your area, and you have heard a request on the radio for young people to show them round. Do you phone up to offer your services?
(a) Yes (b) You think it's a good idea, but never get round to it (c) No

Scoring: (a) = 2 (b) = 1 (c) = 0
6–12: You seem to be adventurous and to enjoy life – yes?
3–6: Maybe you sometimes feel a bit shy or uncertain; does this stop you enjoying yourself as much as you might?
0–3: Maybe you secretly would love to do all those things. Is there someone in your family who has taught you to say 'no' to excitement and adventure?

Crazy ideas list

☐ Go on an all-night hike

☐ Have a midnight feast, with a campfire, friends, etc

☐ Ask your mum or dad to tell you the story of their lives

☐ Have a sauna or a massage

☐ Get up before dawn, walk or cycle out of town and watch the sun come up

☐ Write some poems

☐ Have a party, where everyone brings something to eat, and each person thinks of something interesting, silly or amusing that you all then do

☐ Find out what meetings are on locally and go to one, just to see what it is like

☐ Go canoeing, caving, rock-climbing

Star-rating: *Give the ideas stars, from 5 to 0, depending on how much you like each idea.*

Do something different

What could you do this week that would be different, and enjoyable? Think of something that you would like to do (perhaps something you have never done before) and plan to do it this week. Write it in the space here:

*** Just how important is it to you to enjoy your life, and have a good time?

☐ Very important   ☐ Not very important

☐ Quite important   ☐ Not important

302. 094

EM02114

How do you view life in general?

For instructions, see next page.

	A	B	C

☐ ☐ ☐ 1 'If you work hard, you can achieve most things.'
Agree/disagree/sometimes true

☐ ☐ ☐ 2 'You have to be rich to get what you want in life.'
Agree/disagree/partly true

☐ ☐ ☐ 3 'What matters in life is not "success", but being happy and being kind to other people.'
Agree/disagree/both matter

☐ ☐ ☐ 4 'Life is a struggle, and you have to fight to succeed.'
Agree/disagree/partly true

☐ ☐ ☐ 5 'If you have a negative attitude towards life, everything will seem to be difficult.'
Agree/disagree/partly true

☐ ☐ ☐ 6 'If you have a positive attitude towards life, life may still be difficult, but it will be more enjoyable.'
Agree/disagree/maybe true sometimes

☐ ☐ ☐ 7 'There is no chance in life for young people these days.'
Agree/disagree

☐ ☐ ☐ 8 'There is no point in bothering, because what's the point?'
Agree/disagree

☐ ☐ ☐ 9 'The rich have got it all sewn up. There's no room for us.'
Agree/disagree/partly true

☐ ☐ ☐ 10 'The world is in a terrible mess.'
Agree/disagree/partly agree

☐ ☐ ☐ 11 'It is up to us young people to find a better way of living on this earth, because the adults certainly aren't making a very good job of it.'
Agree/disagree/agree sometimes

☐ ☐ ☐ 12 'Why should I care about other people? I've got enough problems of my own.'
Agree/disagree/agree sometimes

☐ ☐ ☐ 13 'The world was only ever changed by people believing that they could change it.'
Agree/disagree/agree sometimes

☐ ☐ ☐ 14 'If only I felt there was some hope for the world as a whole, I might make a bit of an effort.'
Agree/disagree/agree sometimes

☐ ☐ ☐ 15 'People who stand around moaning about how bad life is should get off their backsides and do something about it.'
Agree/disagree

☐ ☐ ☐ 16 'I just feel a bit lost.'
Often feel this way/sometimes feel this way/don't often feel this way

☐ ☐ ☐ 17 'I'm full of ideas and dreams. I just need some support to realise them.'
Often feel this way/sometimes feel this way/never feel this way

☐ ☐ ☐ 18 'No matter what you do as a young person, it's all a waste of time.'
I feel this way most of the time/I sometimes feel this way/I hardly ever feel this way

☐ ☐ ☐ 19 'The world is an amazing and a beautiful place, really. I wish I understood why there was so much fighting, cruelty and suffering in it.'
Often feel this way/sometimes feel this way/never feel this way

☐ ☐ ☐ 20 'Our planet is still a backward and primitive member of the galaxy, really. We need longer to evolve and develop, and then we will learn to live in a much happier and better way.'
Agree/disagree/it's an interesting idea

☐ ☐ ☐ 21 If everyone followed the way of Jesus (Mohammed/Buddha/Krishna/_____, delete whichever you like) there would be no more war or fighting.'
Agree/disagree/not sure

☐ ☐ ☐ 22 'Humans are basically greedy and sinful. You can never change human nature.'
Agree/disagree/not sure

☐ ☐ ☐ 23 'Humans are basically kind and loving. It is ignorance, prejudice and narrow-mindedness which causes a lot of our troubles.'
Agree/disagree/partly agree

☐ ☐ ☐ 24 'When I look up at the stars at night, I feel that there is so much more to life than I understand. It is all so mysterious.'
I often feel this way/I sometimes feel this way/I never feel this way

☐ ☐ ☐ 25

Instructions for page 5

1 Think about each statement, and underline the words following it that express your feelings about it.

2 Write your own statement in the space at the end.

3 Have someone write these 'new' statements up on a board or paper where everyone can see them, giving them numbers.

4 Mark the three statements which you agree with the most by putting a ★ next to them in column A. (Include the newly written statements too, when making your choice.)

5 Find out the views of the group as a whole, by asking each person to read out the three statement numbers which they agree with most, and keeping a tally in column B.

6 Add the totals for everyone for each statement and write the result in column C.

7 What kind of outlook on life do you have?

☐ Basically positive   ☐ Basically negative   ☐ Mixture of both

8 What kind of outlook on life do the members of your group have?

Basically positive _____ (number of people)
Basically negative _____ (number of people)
Mixture of both _____ (number of people)

9 What effect do you think that this has on the atmosphere, mood and morale in your group?

Action-learning

★ Either use this list of statements, or make up your own, and find out what the opinions of other young people are:
● on the streets   ● on YTS schemes   ● on Community Programme schemes
● in colleges   ● or in schools.

★ Arrange a meeting with the editor of your local paper, or, if possible, with the director of the local radio station, and write an article or produce a programme about young people's views of life.

Radio stations and local newspapers

★ In several places in this book, as here, the suggestion is made that young people might either approach a local radio station and offer to make a short programme, or approach a local newspaper editor and offer to write an article.

The author's experience is that local media like to show that they are involved in local activities and that they like anything that is 'different'. The reason why we do not often hear radio programmes produced by young people is that young people hardly ever go to the radio stations and ask. If two or three members of your group arrange to set up a meeting with one of the radio producers, or with a local editor, you will set up a relationship, from which other developments can follow. In some places, you may get a straight 'no'; in others, you may get a lot of interest. First, try and arrange a meeting, and then see what happens.

Even if your article is not published or your programme is not broadcast, you will still gain from the experience of drawing your observations and views together in a particular format.

Feeling positive

Some people are very positive. They see the bright side of everything. They give encouragement and praise to other people. They smile and laugh a lot.
Agree/disagree/partly true

Other people are more negative. They put a downer on bright ideas and on idealism. They are quick to criticise and slow to praise. They moan about life and say how bad the world is all the time.
Agree/disagree/partly true

As newborn children we are born filled with positive energy. We want to live, to eat, to love, to crawl, to

explore. We are eager to learn.
Agree/disagree/partly true

Many people don't live their lives to the full. They live half-lives, feeling 'I'm not good enough to do that' or 'I wish I could do that', or just feeling bored all the time.

Why do some people only live half-lives? Tick the reasons below that seem important in column A, and then put a second tick next to the single reason which you think is the most important, in column B.

A   B

☐ ☐ They watch too much television

☐ ☐ School has that kind of effect on you

☐ ☐ Being at home has that kind of effect on you

☐ ☐ There is 'nothing happening' where they live

☐ ☐ They don't have the courage to get up and go, and do things

☐ ☐ They don't have any ideas, and they don't have proper information about things that they could do

☐ ☐ They mix with friends who also live dull lives

☐ ☐ Their parents live dull, uninteresting lives

☐ ☐ They get 'fixed' by a general feeling of boredom, and feel that everything is meaningless, which means that they never really *do* anything – they just *talk* about doing things

☐ ☐ They don't believe that it is worth making an effort, because they don't believe that anything good can come of it

☐ ☐ They have been told what to do by other people too much, and so now they want to prove their own freedom by doing nothing

☐ ☐ They believe that the world is going to be blown up in a nuclear war anyway – so what's the point?

☐ ☐ They have grown used to life being boring while at school, and have never discovered how exciting it can be

☐ ☐ They have lived too much in grey concrete neighbourhoods, where there is nothing to do but kick old tins around and get into trouble

Creating positive energy

Six activities guaranteed to bring positive energy into the group:

1   Clear a large space in the room, and play three quick games of 'tag' in succession. First game's rules: Whenever you are caught you have to stand with your legs apart, until someone frees you by crawling through them. Second game's rules: You are only safe from being caught when you are hugging one other person, for a maximum count of five. Third game's rules: Everyone (tagging pair included) works in pairs, arms around each other, and has to stay together.

2   Do a group 'brainstorm' to find '30 ways in which we could improve our club/school/YTS scheme'. All ideas get written down; none get criticised. Do a warm-up brainstorm first, to find 30 ways to use one old boot.

3   Break up into small groups of three or four people, and create a series of three challenges that the other groups have to do, as groups, without leaving the room, and without involving anything indecent or dangerous. You must be prepared to do the challenges yourselves, as a group, if asked.

4   Plan a 'stunt' which you will do together within the next 24 hours (nothing illegal, immoral, etc).

5   Go into town in pairs with a clipboard and notepad each, and interview people about 'the best and the worst things that ever happened to them', writing down their responses. Then bring the results back, and share them with the rest of the group.

6   Based on your brainstorm above, draw up a list of serious changes that you would like to see made in your club/school/YTS scheme, and take it to your director/head/manager, etc.

What makes you feel positive?

	A	B	C	
	☐	☐	☐	1 Having lots of fun
	☐	☐	☐	2 Doing things that are different
	☐	☐	☐	3 Having good friends
	☐	☐	☐	4 Doing something that I enjoy doing
	☐	☐	☐	5 Having people who trust me and believe in me
	☐	☐	☐	6 Achieving a good piece of work
	☐	☐	☐	7 Keeping fit and healthy
	☐	☐	☐	8 Being able to talk openly and honestly with people
	☐	☐	☐	9 Doing something that I believe in
	☐	☐	☐	10
	☐	☐	☐	11
	☐	☐	☐	12
	☐	☐	☐	13
	☐	☐	☐	14
	☐	☐	☐	15

1 Add further things that make you feel positive in the spaces, and write them up on a board where others can see them too, giving them numbers from 10 upwards. Copy any which you like onto your sheet, with their numbers, in the spaces 10–15.

2 Put a ★ in column A next to each thing that helps you to feel positive.

3 Put a second ★ in column B, next to the three things that help you the most to feel positive.

4 Now use column C to build up a group score, showing what makes you feel positive.

Dealing with difficulties

★ Before you start this section: How are you feeling now? Circle how you feel on this scale:

Lousy 0 1 2 3 4 5 6 7 8 9 10 Great

Group total: _____

We are unique and wonderful, but we get into real muddles and messes too. Lots of people's hopes and dreams don't work out. Why? Why is life so difficult?

Philosophers, magicians and priests have tried to answer that question for centuries. Let's leave it aside, and ask a more direct question:

What are the main difficulties that you experience in your own life at the moment?

Score each item on the list 0, 1, 2 or 3, in column A.
0 = not a difficulty at all   2 = quite a big difficulty
1 = a small difficulty   3 = a major difficulty

	A	B	
	☐	☐	Boredom
	☐	☐	Arguments and fights with friends
	☐	☐	Racism and prejudice
	☐	☐	Lack of money
	☐	☐	Don't like the area I live in
	☐	☐	Lack of self-confidence

☐ ☐	Emotional turmoil	
☐ ☐	Not getting on with my parents	
☐ ☐	Inner anger and violence	
☐ ☐	Not liking the work that I am doing	
☐ ☐	Lack of emotional support	
☐ ☐	Arguments and fights in the family	
☐ ☐	Not knowing what to do with my life	
☐ ☐	Not getting on with my teachers and supervisors	
☐ ☐	Travel difficulties	
☐ ☐	Not finding any good friends	
☐ ☐	Not finding any close personal friends	
☐ ☐	Shyness	
☐ ☐	Feeling overweight	
☐ ☐	Health problems	
☐ ☐	Fear of nuclear war	
☐ ☐	Lack of hope for the future, personally	
☐ ☐	Lack of hope for the future of the world, generally	
☐ ☐	Bullies	
☐ ☐	Hating school/training course	
☐ ☐	Drugs/drink problems	
☐ ☐	Sexual harassment	
☐ ☐	Men	
☐ ☐	Women	
☐ ☐	Unemployment	
☐ ☐	Atmosphere of boredom among my friends	
☐ ☐	Lack of a good place to live	
☐ ☐	Not being able to read or write properly	
☐ ☐	The way people react to me	
☐ ☐	Relationship difficulties	

☐ ☐ Sex

☐ ☐ Harassment on the streets

☐ ☐ Getting stuck in a negative attitude

☐ ☐

☐ ☐

☐ ☐

☐ ☐

When you have finished, check how you are feeling again:

Lousy 0 1 2 3 4 5 6 7 8 9 10 Great

Group total: _____

Has your score changed? Has the group's total score changed? The 'feelings' scores may all have fallen.

Negative ideas produce negative feelings.
Negative feelings produce negative ideas — unless you choose to change.

It is possible to get caught in this circle, and go around feeling lousy for days, weeks or even *years* on end.

Action-learning

● Group exercise – how can you build up a wider picture of the difficulties which the young people in your group are experiencing, without intruding on people's individual privacy? Some of the difficulties that people experience are very personal, and they don't like other people to know that they experience them.

● Work out a way in which you can find out what your group members have scored in total for each difficulty, without anyone being able to know what an individual person has written. (Use column B for this purpose.)

● Write a short press release describing your findings, and then contact a local radio or TV station, and try and persuade them to hold a discussion about young people's problems.

How do you respond to the difficulties?

Everyone experiences difficulty.

Some people experience **huge** difficulties. Other people experience smaller difficulties.

No one on the whole earth lives a life that is free of difficulties.

The big difference between people is **how we respond to difficulties**.

There are at least five common **negative responses** to difficulty:

	A	B
1 Getting angry, fighting, feeling cross	☐	☐
2 Blaming people – judgements, racism, bullying, hatred	☐	☐
3 Avoidance – running away, drugs, drink	☐	☐
4 Avoidance – ignoring it, and hoping it will go away	☐	☐
5 Withdrawal – self-blame, self-criticism, depression	☐	☐
6	☐	☐

And many possible **positive responses** to difficulty:

7 Discussing the problem, and talking about it with the people involved	☐	☐
8 Organising with other people who experience the same difficulty to find ways to overcome the problem	☐	☐
9 Developing personal strength and courage to 'pick yourself up', smile, and carry on in spite of the difficulties	☐	☐
10 Ignoring the difficulties, and putting energy instead into new positive activities, in order to develop a happy and enjoyable side to your life	☐	☐
11 Finding a good friend who will listen while you share your worries	☐	☐
12 Choosing to change what you are doing, or to do things differently in future	☐	☐
13	☐	☐
14	☐	☐

How do **you** deal with your difficulties?

Choose one of your current difficulties, and place a tick in column A showing which method you usually use to deal with it. If you need to add to the list, use the spaces to do so.

Now choose two more difficulties and do the same, using column A again.

As a group, build up a picture of how you respond to difficulties. When each person has three ticks, use column B to show the group total for each way of responding to difficulty.

Why is this important?
All through life, you will meet difficulties. Some people say, 'Don't worry: the first 100 years are the worst'.

If you do not overcome difficulties, they will overcome you.

Throughout centuries of life, people have struggled with difficulties. Many people have found ways to overcome them, and have managed to realise their dreams. Many others have not. Developing positive ways to overcome your difficulties is **essential** if you want to realise your dreams.

● How do your parents deal with their difficulties? Take these pages home to them, and ask them to fill in the same exercises.

● How do the adults in your school/college/scheme/ project deal with their difficulties? Use the exercises as a questionnaire with them.

What do you hope for in life?

The mathematics of success: eight steps

A

☐ ● Long-term hopes and dreams

☐ ● Short-term, clear, practical objectives

☐ ● A positive attitude

☐ ● Plans

☐ ● Actions and hard work

☐ ● A willingness to help others and ask for help

☐ ● Persistence

☐ ● An ability to overcome problems and difficulties as they arise

Realisation of your dreams

There are eight factors above which are necessary if people are to realise their hopes and dreams. Which are the most important? Place them in order from one to eight, in column A, as you see their importance.

Now decide what you think about these three statements:

● In past years, only a few people were able to realise their hopes and dreams. Most people had to do routine, semi-skilled work in factories, shops and offices, or on the land. Agree/disagree/not sure

● Automation and the microprocessor are now taking over much more of the routine work. Humans are now free to pursue their own personal hopes in life. Agree/don't agree/not sure

● In order to pursue your hopes, you have first to be clear what they are. Agree/don't agree/not sure

What do you hope for in life?

Have a look at the list below.

A B C

☐ ☐ ☐ Adventure

☐ ☐ ☐ Romance

☐ ☐ ☐ Travel

☐ ☐ ☐ A good job

☐ ☐ ☐ A good career

☐ ☐ ☐ Fulfilment

☐ ☐ ☐ Personal happiness

☐ ☐ ☐ Children and family

☐ ☐ ☐ Excitement

☐ ☐ ☐ Security

☐ ☐ ☐ Money

☐ ☐ ☐ Danger

☐ ☐ ☐ Love

☐ ☐ ☐ Close friendships

☐ ☐ ☐ Opportunities to fight racialism and other kinds of injustice

☐ ☐ ☐ Opportunities to help create a better world, without war, famine or cruelty to animals

☐ ☐ ☐ Opportunities to help other people

☐ ☐ ☐ 'Success'

☐ ☐ ☐ A lovely house to live in, in lovely surroundings

☐ ☐ ☐ Opportunities to be creative, in words, music, art, dance, sculpture, video, film, dance, etc

☐ ☐ ☐ Inner peace and happiness

☐ ☐ ☐

☐ ☐ ☐

☐ ☐ ☐

1 First add on any additional hopes of your own.
2 Place stars by the ones that you hope for in column A.
3 Mark your top five hopes with a ★ in column B.
4 Place them in order from one to five, using column C, so that your greatest hope is no 1.

This is only a broad beginning. What is really needed is a completely personal list of all your hopes and dreams. Having a clear list in your mind will help you to achieve them.

What are your dreams?

This is another look at your hopes and dreams, in a bit more detail: What are your dreams today, as you sit in this room?

Instructions opposite.

A B

☐ ☐ I dream of being able to learn some practical skills which will enable me to earn a living and be useful to other people.

☐ ☐ I dream of being able to travel and to see the world.

☐ ☐ I dream of developing a happy relationship with my parents (or foster – or step parents) and my family, in which there will be plenty of laughter, love and friendship, and no fights, jealousies, hatreds or empty silences.

☐ ☐ I dream of finding someone whom I can love, and be loved by, in a happy relationship.

☐ ☐ I dream of being able to understand myself much better, and of knowing why I am here on the earth.

☐ ☐ I dream of getting a good job and earning lots of money.

☐ ☐ I dream of achieving success/fame through using my skills as a _____.

☐ ☐ I dream of being able to help to abolish war and nuclear weapons, so that we can all live without fear of destruction.

☐ ☐ I dream of being able to do something to help people to live in pleasant houses and communities, in beautiful, safe surroundings.

☐ ☐ I dream of being able to help to prevent all cruelty to children, to animals and to nature.

☐ ☐ I dream of being able to be independent, and to earn my own living, somehow or other.

☐ ☐ I dream of being able to have close, loving friendships, and of there being an end to cruelty, fear and bullying between people.

A B

☐ ☐ I dream of being able to help to end all racism, and of being able to help black and white people to understand and respect each other.

☐ ☐ I dream of having lots of money.

☐ ☐ I dream of going far away from my family and everyone I know, and of starting a new life.

☐ ☐ I dream of being able to read and write properly, and being able to go to college and get a good education.

☐ ☐ I dream of being able to climb mountains, to fly, to go scuba diving, to do free-fall skydiving, to go white-water canoeing, to live with challenge, excitement and adventure.

☐ ☐ I dream of being able to feel good about myself, and being able to love myself, all of the time.

☐ ☐ I dream of being able to pay back all those who have hurt me in one way or another.

☐ ☐ I dream of being an accepted member of a gang, and of making other gangs afraid of us.

☐ ☐ I dream of dying, and ending my life.

☐ ☐ I dream of waking up one morning and finding inner peacefulness and serenity/ stillness, in which I will always be able to see how beautiful the world really is.

☐ ☐ I dream of

> *I'd dare to make more mistakes next time. I'd relax. I would limber up. I would be sillier than I have been this trip. I would climb more mountains and swim more rivers. I would eat more ice creams and less beans. I would perhaps have more actual troubles, but I'd have fewer imaginary ones.*
> *If I had my life to live over again, I would start barefoot earlier in the spring and stay that way later in the autumn. I would go to more dances. I would ride more merry-go-rounds. I would pick more daisies.*
> Nadine Stair, aged 85.

What is 'success'?

1 Put a star next to each dream that means something to you in column A.
2 Stop and think. Add your own dream to the list, giving it a star too.
3 Now choose the three dreams which mean the most to you, marking them with a star in column B.

Think of *one small personal dream* which you carry in your heart, but which you have not done anything about yet. What is your dream?

Your dream: _____

_____

_____

_____

Unless we have dreams, we will never achieve them. A dream is like a star, which you can follow. Simply holding a dream in your mind will help you to achieve it.

You have a choice between:

1 A life based upon what **you** want for yourself

2 A life based on what **other people** want you to do

3 A life not based on anything.

Which do you want? Place a tick after the choice you prefer.

Action-learning

● Use the list on page 12 as a questionnaire, and find out what other young people dream of in your school. You could also use it on the streets, to find out what kind of dreams the general public carries.

● Use your results to hold a discussion on a local radio show, on television, or to write an article in a local paper.

Self-confidence

Building up your own self-confidence is one of the keys to success. It means believing in yourself.

Many people live their lives without much self-confidence. Why do you think this is?

A

☐ ● Lack of encouragement from their parents

☐ ● Having parents who are not self-confident

☐ ● Being hurt by other people saying cruel things

☐ ● Living a sheltered life

☐ ● Lacking practical experience

☐ ● Not being given the chance to do things for themselves

☐ ● Not being given the chance to make mistakes, without it mattering

☐ ● Some people will never be self-confident

☐ ● Being oppressed by other people, or by society

☐ ● Not being loved enough when young

☐ ●

1 Think of some people whom you know who appear to lack self-confidence.
2 Think why they may lack self-confidence.
3 Place three stars in column A by the three reasons which you think are the most important reasons why people lose self-confidence.

Remember: We are all incredible human beings. Nothing can ever change that.

What do you think you need to make a success of your life?

'You've got to be willing to walk on other people, in order to get to the top.' True/false

'If you've got lots of friends in high places, you can succeed.' True/false

'Being successful at what you want to do is simply a matter of personal determination.' True/false

'If you haven't got some good skills, you'll never succeed.' True/false

'You can't get anywhere these days without qualifications.' True/false

'The main thing that matters if you want to succeed is having a positive attitude towards life.' True/false

'If you are willing to learn from others, you can go a long way.' True/false

'If you've got money, you can get a long way in life.' True/false

'Some people will never succeed, no matter what help you give them.' True/false

'People who believe in themselves are generally able to reach their goals in life.' True/false

'The same things that make a person succeed in life can make the same person make a success of unemployment.' True/false

'If you do what you are told, you will succeed in life.' True/false

'If you want to succeed, you have to fight, fight, fight.' True/false

'If you know what you want really clearly, you stand a good chance of getting it.' True/false

'Everyone is born capable of success.' True/false

What is 'success'?

1 'Success is being able to do whatever you want in life.' True/false

2 'Success is being able to achieve your goals.' True/false

3 'Success is being famous.' True/false

4 'Success is having lots of money.' True/false

5 'Success means something different to each person.' True/false

6 'People who are successful are very often unhappy.' True/false

7 'People who are rich and famous are very often unhappy.' True/false

8 'What is a big "success" to one person might seem like nothing to another.' True/false

9 'For someone who is alcoholic, not drinking for a whole day is success.' True/false

10 'It isn't "success" that matters in life. It is being happy, and making other people happy.' True/false

In your own opinion, which statements are true and which are false?

Which three statements do you agree with the most strongly?
Numbers _____/_____/_____

Now write below what your own definition of 'success' is:

_____

_____

_____

One woman's way to 'success'
Letter from Mandy King

May 1986

'I became unemployed in 1981 after leaving what I found to be a repetitive and undemanding job in a small electrical factory in the rural village where I had grown up. I decided the village had nothing to offer me and vice versa, so I moved in with a friend in the nearest town, Ipswich. At this point, unskilled and unqualified, I soon lost hope in the prospects of employment and resigned myself to a life on the dole.

I became homeless and a group of homeless unemployed people I knew were squatting in empty houses, so I moved into a squat with them. They also had little hope of becoming employed, and some of them were highly skilled. Drugs became a way of life escalating from smoking at parties to playing around with hallucinogenics, just to pass the time.

Meditating
The changes in my attitude came when I became a vegetarian and met a friend who taught me to meditate. I became very aware of what I had been doing and how my mind was decomposing, making me lethargic and forgetful. I broke away from the group of friends and found myself a shared house and stopped taking drugs. Having rented accommodation gave me a secure background, no more moving from one place to another sometimes after two days of being somewhere.

Group activities
A friend told me about the unemployment group at Stonelodge and outlined the activities they planned, so I went along. Different activities were set for each day of three days a week, which stimulated me to carry on going at first. Jenny and Caroline, the girls who ran it, impressed me because I didn't know too many women who had careers and families too. I found them very easy to talk to, and discussion groups amongst the group stimulated my long-dormant mind.

We were encouraged to take part in crafts, sports, cookery, computing and video filming. I soon became a regular member of the group and outside those three days I was stimulated to do more things to stop myself becoming bored until the next group session started.

On a Wednesday the group started canoeing lessons at Cattawade. I'll never forget how terrified I was of a canoe and was sure I'd capsize, never to escape, but Wendy, the instructress, was very encouraging, and, after a wobbly start, I became quite a confident canoeist and was celebrating achievement in an area that previously seemed out of my range of physical ability.

Self-awareness exercises in the group really helped to get myself into perspective and were food for thought.

Responsibility
We would prepare "group" lunches every day, for visitors too, and cooked vegetarian meals. I really enjoyed cooking and creative work. At first Jenny and Caroline instigated the lunches; then, as they had more and more paperwork, they gave me more responsibility and I thrived on it; it had been so long since I had been in a position of trust. I found myself no longer pessimistic about the future but enjoying new developments every day.

Caroline arrived at Stonelodge with the Health Express magazine one day which had an advertisement for applicants interested in a vegetarian catering course. I wrote off to the girl in question and she posted me on an application form for Plymouth College.

I'm now at the end of my first year and have enjoyed the challenge of continuous assessments in academic and practical subjects. Looking back at the last five years I feel a sense of awakening and total change in attitude. The unemployment group project was an important influence, teaching how to apply skills and renew confidence. Being a woman, I found the professional women I met became of major importance to my development. They proved that it is worth persevering, that being a mother and wife is no longer the only future a woman has to resign her talents to.'

(With thanks to Mandy King and Caroline London, in Ipswich)

Who supports/discourages you?

Some people give us good words – praise, encouragement, support. This gives us confidence, and helps us to believe in ourselves. They fill up our teapot.

Who are the people close to you who give you good words? Fill in their names in the spaces just below.

Other people give us criticism. We are never good enough for them. We are always doing something wrong. Or perhaps they simply never say anything encouraging, which feels like a discouragement. The comments that these people make are like holes in the same teapot, and our self-confidence drains away through them.

Do you have any people like this in your life? If you do, write their names in the spaces just above.

Why do some people give lots of encouragement, and others give criticism?
Is it possible to give both?
Is it possible that they were never given any encouragement themselves?

How much time do you spend with the 'encouragers', and how much with the 'criticisers'? Can you perhaps spend more time with the people who make you feel good about yourself?

How full is your pot?

Having a 'full pot' means that you feel plenty of encouragement, you feel self-confident, and you feel good about yourself (high 'self-esteem'). Is your pot:

Full?   ¾ full?   ½ full?   ¼ full?   Empty?

Do **you** give encouragement and support to people?   Yes ☐ No ☐ Sometimes ☐

Who would you like to give more encouragement and support to? Write their names here:

1 _____   3 _____   5 _____
2 _____   4 _____   6 _____

What kind of supports do you have?

In order for us to realise our dreams, it is helpful (but not necessary) to have external supports. Hardly anyone has **all** the supports listed below. Which ones do **you** have?

Step 1: Read through each possible support, and place a tick in either column A or column B.
Step 2: Which supports could you build up for yourself? Place a star in column C for each one.
Note: Each support is worth one tick unless otherwise indicated.

	I have this support already	I lack this support	I could build up this support for myself	My 3 most important supports
	A	B	C	D
Material supports:				
Good physical health (scores 2 ticks in box A or B)	☐	☐	☐	☐
A dry, warm house to live in (scores 2)	☐	☐	☐	☐
A good diet, healthy food	☐	☐	☐	☐
A room or flat of my own where I can feel free to do as I like	☐	☐	☐	☐
Emotional supports:				
At least one person who loves me and supports me, whatever I do (scores 2)	☐	☐	☐	☐
A warm, supportive atmosphere in my home, full of laughter and happiness (scores 2)	☐	☐	☐	☐
People I can talk to (and cry with if need be) and share my feelings, thoughts and worries with (scores 2)	☐	☐	☐	☐
People I can get angry with, without risk of losing their love or friendship	☐	☐	☐	☐
Plenty of physical contact and touch (scores 2)	☐	☐	☐	☐
Community supports:				
Freedom from racism, prejudice and harassment locally	☐	☐	☐	☐
Streets that are safe to walk on, locally	☐	☐	☐	☐
A good community centre and advice centre	☐	☐	☐	☐
A place where young people can meet to do things together without interference	☐	☐	☐	☐
Trees, parks and quiet places, locally	☐	☐	☐	☐
Mental supports:				
Friendship with people whom I can hold intelligent discussions with	☐	☐	☐	☐
Support for reading books, watching educational TV films, and thinking about life, society and the world	☐	☐	☐	☐
Spiritual and cultural supports:				
Opportunities to express myself creatively through the arts, dance, music, etc	☐	☐	☐	☐
A set of beliefs that enable me to believe that life is worth living and that the difficulties are worth overcoming (scores 2)	☐	☐	☐	☐
Economic supports:				
Money enough to buy clothes, shoes, books, materials, equipment and bus fares	☐	☐	☐	☐
A choice of good training, educational openings, jobs and careers	☐	☐	☐	☐

Total:
(Maximum 30)

Which supports do you think are the most important to help you realise your dreams? In column D, choose the three supports which you feel are most important for you, and mark them with a star.

16

What stops you?

What stops you from:

- [ ] Getting in a school/YTS/local sports team?
- [ ] Earning spare-time money by, eg, cleaning cars?
- [ ] Making your own clothes?
- [ ] Travelling away from home on your own?
- [ ] Doing well at your studies?
- [ ] Forming a band?
- [ ] Joining a group such as Friends of the Earth?
- [ ] Joining a keep-fit/aerobics class?
- [ ] Achieving all of your dreams?

★ = Nothing
O = Fears, uncertainties
? = Don't know

Action-learning

★ Choose *one thing* that you have never done before which you would like to do, which would be challenging, and *do it in the coming week.*

Use a group method to generate a list of things people might never have done before, and then choose your projects. Take on projects singly, or in pairs.

Ideas list (just to stimulate your imagination):

Ice-skate	Take a sauna	Be a member of
Climb a mountain	Have a massage	TV studio
Write some poetry	Go riding	audience
Go to a concert	Take up a new sport	Tour a local factory
Do a day's work with someone local	Raise £25 for Oxfam	Walk/run x miles
Earning some money		Do some voluntary work at the local hospital

Buried wishes

Do you have some buried wishes? These might help you to think of things to do during the week. Complete this sentence, three times:

'I have always wanted to: _____'

'I have always wanted to: _____'

'I have always wanted to: _____'

Examples: 'I have always wanted to work in a radio studio.' Possible/impossible/unlikely
'I have always wanted to look at the stars through a proper telescope.' Possible/impossible/unlikely
'I have always wanted to go up in a hot-air balloon.' Possible/impossible/unlikely
'I have always wanted to take my mum for a day out.' Possible/impossible/unlikely

Make a large group list of your buried wishes, and then see if you can build them into your plans for the week.

Our favourite excuses

Very often, we make excuses instead of doing what we know that we *can* do, if we honour our dreams. If Bob Geldof had made excuses instead of acting on his dream, Bandaid, Liveaid and Sportaid would never have happened, and millions more people would have starved to death in Africa.

So what are *your* favourite excuses for not doing things? We all make excuses not to do things that we find challenging – every one of us. In the list below, tick the excuses which you know that you use, in column A:

A	B	
[ ]	[ ]	'I don't need any excuses – I can do anything I want'
[ ]	[ ]	'I don't know how to do it'
[ ]	[ ]	'I am shy with people'
[ ]	[ ]	'I'm not good enough'
[ ]	[ ]	'Nobody is supporting me'
[ ]	[ ]	'I'm too busy doing other things'
[ ]	[ ]	'I haven't fed the cat'
[ ]	[ ]	'I might make a fool of myself'
[ ]	[ ]	'I might make a mistake'
[ ]	[ ]	'I don't have anyone to encourage me'
[ ]	[ ]	'It's too much effort'
[ ]	[ ]	'I don't know who to ask for information'
[ ]	[ ]	'I've never done it before'
[ ]	[ ]	'I don't know anyone else who is doing it'
[ ]	[ ]	'It's easier not to bother'
[ ]	[ ]	'Maybe I'll do it next week/next year'
[ ]	[ ]	'I'm nervous'

When you have filled in your own personal excuses, find out which are the most popular excuses, and fill in the group score for each excuse, in column B.

Then for this week, write up a large notice, saying **I can, I will, nothing need stop me.**

Your personal power

What does 'having power' mean to you?
(Tick the ones you feel 'yes' to):

☐ Telling other people what to do

☐ Being 'the leader', and having other people listen to me

☐ Being able to do as I like in my life, without other people telling me what to do

☐ Being able to choose what I do for myself, and doing it

☐ Taking full responsibility for my own life

☐ Being a 'star', appearing on stage

☐ Being able to reach my own goals

☐ Feeling good about myself, feeling confident

☐ Being an MP or an 'important person'

☐ Having wealth and posh things

1 'Having personal power means being able to have power over other people.' Agree/disagree

2 'Having personal power means being able to act upon my own dreams and goals.' Agree/disagree

3 'Having personal power means being fully in charge of my own life, and not living it the way someone else wants.' Agree/disagree

4 'It is natural that some people should be leaders, and tell others what to do.' Agree/disagree

5 'People who want to have power over other people are dangerous. Having personal power is about having power over my own life, not over other people's lives.' Agree/disagree

Your personal power – do you abuse it?
Text from the *Sacred Tree* book from the Four Worlds Development Project, University of Lethbridge, Alberta, Canada, with grateful acknowledgements.

What stops you from 'having power'?
(Tick the ones that are true for you):

☐ Lack of confidence in myself

☐ The belief that I'm just not a born leader

☐ Parents, teachers, other adults

☐ 'The System'

☐ Lack of practice at doing what I want to do for myself

☐ Nothing

☐ Simply my youth: give me time, and I will claim my own personal power

Every time you overrule your excuses, and do something that you want to do, you increase your personal power.

The ways by which people try to dominate others or demonstrate selfishness may be defined in two ways: the active, obvious ways, and the less active, more indirect ways. Among the active, obvious ways are the use of physical force, bullying, boasting, temper tantrums, and excessive noisiness. These obvious ways are easily identified. It is the use of the less obvious methods that we often fail to realise that the real purpose of our behaviour is to compel another person to do what we want.

The following is a partial list of questions we should occasionally ask ourselves in order to guard against the subtle attitudes of selfishness and the feeling that we must get our own way.

The only reason we ever act in these ways is because we have been hurt, and are trying to get rid of those feelings; one common way is to act out our hurts on others, instead of choosing safe and appropriate places to deal with them.

1 Do I frequently find fault with others, with members of my family, friends, or those with whom I work? If I do, why am I so sure that my own way of feeling, thinking and acting is so much better than theirs? Yes, often/yes, sometimes/no

2 Do I engage in backbiting? The dictionary defines backbiting as 'speaking negatively about those who are not present'. Yes, often/yes, sometimes/no

3 Do I listen to backbiting and by so doing encourage this characteristic in another person? Yes, often/yes, sometimes/no

4 Do I talk so much that I deprive others of the opportunity to express their knowledge and ideas? Yes, often/yes, sometimes/no

5 Do I talk too little, depriving others of my ideas, experience and knowledge? Yes, often/yes, sometimes/no

6 Do I speak with a too-loud and intimidating voice? Yes, often/yes, sometimes/no

7 Do I speak with a murmur, so that others have to strain or sometimes are not able to hear what I have to say? Yes, often/yes, sometimes/no

8 Am I argumentative, quarrelsome or defensive when presenting my ideas? Yes, often/yes, sometimes/no

9 Do I use sarcasm, hurting the feelings of others with my cutting remarks? (Of all the verbal techniques for dominating people, sarcasm is probably the most cruel.) Yes, often/yes, sometimes/no

10 Do I whine and complain? Which may say to the listener, 'See how weak I am! You must take care of me and see to it that I get what I want'. Yes, often/yes, sometimes/no

11 Do I sulk, holding myself aloof in a sullen, ill-humoured or offended mood? This is a subtle way of manipulating others. Yes, often/yes, sometimes/no

12 Do I express my feelings of discouragement, depression or sadness in ways which darken the lives of others instead of lightening my own burden? Yes, often/yes, sometimes/no

13 Am I always late for appointments? If so, am I really saying to the individual or group kept waiting for me, 'Your time is less valuable than mine, so it doesn't matter if I waste some of your time; you should be willing to wait on my convenience?'. Yes, often/yes, sometimes/no

14 Do I break my promises? Yes, often/yes, sometimes/no

15 Am I frequently indecisive saying, 'Do whatever you like: either way is all right with me; I really don't have any preference'? Yes, often/yes, sometimes/no

16 Do I make an overly boastful display of my intelligence, my attainments, or my possessions? Do I 'show off' so I can make it clear that I wish to 'separate' myself from others? Yes, often/yes, sometimes/no

17 Do I show contempt for the feelings, ideas or actions of others? Yes, often/yes, sometimes/no

18 Do I demand special privileges, so that others are deprived? Do I expect to have the most comfortable chair, the most honoured seat at a gathering or the highest position in any group or organisation to which I belong? Yes, often/yes, sometimes/no

19 Do I dislike another person because that person shows a character trait of my own, which I am trying to ignore in myself? If I express an intense dislike for greediness, is it because I am really a greedy person myself? Yes, often/yes, sometimes/no

20 Am I always asking myself the question: 'What will other people say?' Yes, often/yes, sometimes/no

Personal goals and strategies

Her dream

Rachel, aged 17, is in a fix. She argued with her parents six months ago, and stormed out of the house. She is unemployed, and is not enjoying life in Birmingham. She wants to go home.

To be able to live with my parents in Gateshead, 200 miles away.

1 See your dream clearly.

2 Break it down into individual goals.

3 Deal with your emotional reactions.

4 Draw up an action plan for each goal.

5 And then take it one step at a time.

Obstacles

1 They won't speak to me.
2 I can't afford to travel to see them.
3 They won't let me live with them unless I have a job.
4 There is very high unemployment in Gateshead.

Emotional result: I feel stuck, and unable to do anything.

How strongly do I want to do anything about it? (Scale 0–10): 10
(A score of less than 7 does not produce energy to fulfil the dream.)

Goal (1): To get back on speaking terms with them.

Emotional reaction (1): Fear that they might reject me.

Emotional reply (1): Well, at least I'll know that I've tried; and I'll have to carry on without them.

Action plan (1): Send them a nice gift by post, and write them a letter.

Goal (2): To raise the money to go and visit them.

Emotional reaction (2): Nobody's got any money – so how can I hope to raise any?

Emotional reply (2): I can always prove them wrong.

Action plan (2): (a) Work out how much is required
(b) Work out how much I could save each week from my present income
(c) Ask everyone I know if they have any small jobs which I could do, to earn the money
(i) Make a list of everyone I know
(ii) Plan when I am going to ask each of them

Goal (3): To find a job in Gateshead.

Emotional reaction (3): Hopelessness – seems useless to begin trying. Unemployment there is very high.

Emotional reply (3): If I become very organised, and get the best advice, I'm sure I can find something. At least I will have done my best.

Action plan (3): (a) Visit the local Careers Office, and ask for the best advice on how to find a job. Ask them for contacts in Gateshead.

(b) Ask them if there are opportunities open to me apart from a regular job – any special training schemes, for instance?

(c) Write to the Careers Service in Gateshead myself, asking for contacts and advice, and asking if I can visit them.

(d) Visit the local Jobcentre, and ask them for advice and contacts, too.

(e) Get hold of a good book on job-hunting, and make sure that I am doing everything properly – my application letters, application forms, interview techniques etc.

What kind of support will I need while doing this?

1 Emotional support from a good friend.

Where can I get this from?

Lizzie – if I ask her, and tell her what I'm trying to do.

2 Practical support with my job-hunting.

Where can I get this from?

Don't know. Will try asking at the Careers Service, and if they can't help, ask them who *can* help.

Results:

Rachel wrote to her parents and sent them a gift, but didn't get a reply. But when she phoned them up, they were a bit more friendly. She couldn't save any money, but she raised £12 doing some sewing for people at the Youth Club, and was able to get a bus to Gateshead. She called on the Careers Service, and they were able to fit her into a one-year Youth Training Scheme working with young children. Now that she has something to do, her parents are willing to have her back with them.

Rachel's plan, shown here, shows how it is possible to turn a big problem, or dream, into a series of small steps, which can lead to the realisation of the dream.

Working and learning

What are your assumptions about people and about the way they work and learn?

True	False			True	False
☐	☐	1 People have to be told what to do in order to learn anything	2 The desire to learn is completely natural in human beings, and doesn't need forcing	☐	☐
☐	☐	3 People don't like to take responsibility. They prefer someone else to take the decisions, and to be told what to do	4 When people are given responsibility, they become responsible people	☐	☐
☐	☐	5 The only way to make a child learn is to force it to learn	6 Children love learning. They just need encouragement and praise	☐	☐
☐	☐	7 People naturally resist change. They prefer to stay in the old ruts	8 People get bored with monotonous routines. They want new experiences	☐	☐
☐	☐	9 Most people dislike working, and will avoid it if they can	10 People love working hard when they enjoy what they are doing	☐	☐
☐	☐	11 Only a few people are naturally creative	12 All people are naturally creative. It just needs encouraging	☐	☐
☐	☐	13 Some young people make trouble at school because that is just the way they are	14 Some young people make trouble at school to be more exciting and creative	☐	☐
☐	☐	15 You can't change human nature	16 All humans can learn, grow and change. They just need encouragement	☐	☐
☐	☐	17 Life is boring	18 Life is only boring if you don't make an effort, and if you have no dreams or goals that you want to achieve	☐	☐

Total **true** answers on **this** side:

Total **true** answers on **this** side:

Which side of the page carries the statements which are true for *you* personally (ie are *you* naturally lazy, or hardworking, etc)? Left side, Right side

True	False			True	False
☐	☐	1 Some people are naturally lazy, irresponsible, are only interested in money and have to be told what to do. Others are gifted with intelligence and creativity and easily take responsibility	2 When people are treated as lazy, irresponsible and inferior, they become so. And when they are treated as responsible, intelligent and creative, they become so	☐	☐

Yes	No			Yes	No
☐	☐	Do the staff/supervisors in your school/scheme/project/youth group see young people as basically lazy, irresponsible and bothersome?	Do the staff/supervisors in your school/scheme/project/youth group see young people as basically intelligent, creative and responsible?	☐	☐

Acknowledgements are made to the *A Must For Youth* CEIC Outreach group in Sydney, Nova Scotia, Canada for ideas used on this page.

Your choices – YTS True or False

The Youth Training Scheme

One of your choices when you leave school is joining the Youth Training Scheme, in order to develop practical, useful skills.

These three pages look at different aspects of YTS.

True False

☐ ☐ 1 You can work for a recognised vocational qualification while you are on YTS

☐ ☐ 2 In 1986, 135,000 young people took up places on YTS

☐ ☐ 3 It is not possible to do a YTS training in farming or agriculture

☐ ☐ 4 YTS trainees get two weeks' holiday a year

☐ ☐ 5 If you leave a YTS scheme 'without good reason', your supplementary benefit may be reduced by 40% for 13 weeks

☐ ☐ 6 Butlin's holiday camps run residential courses for YTS trainees, during which they can do archery, fencing, abseiling, judo and aerobics

☐ ☐ 7 YTS is really just the same as school

☐ ☐ 8 It is possible to train as a police cadet on YTS

☐ ☐ 9 The way you learn things in YTS is very different from the way you learn things at school

☐ ☐ 10 The pay on YTS is £25 a week

☐ ☐ 11 It is possible to run a business while on YTS

☐ ☐ 12 There are over 170 special Information Technology Centres, training some 7,500 YTS trainees in electronics, computing and modern office skills

☐ ☐ 13 It is possible to train to be a Member of Parliament while on YTS

☐ ☐ 14 It is possible to train to be a doctor while on YTS

☐ ☐ 15 It is not possible to join a trade union when you are on YTS

☐ ☐ 16 The staff at the Careers Service keep all the details about places on YTS schemes

☐ ☐ 17 All trainees on YTS learn these basic 'core skills' – road safety, contraception, self-defence, how to fit a plug, how to fix a leaking tap

☐ ☐ 18 All trainees on YTS learn these basic 'core skills' – numbers, communication, problem-solving, practical, computer and information technology

☐ ☐ 19 It is possible to learn falconry on some YTS schemes

☐ ☐ 20 YTS training helps trainees to have a happier love-life

(Answers on page 47)

There is often much confusion or misunderstanding about the YTS, and following this quiz, a group discussion about individuals' attitudes and ideas on the Youth Training Scheme would be valuable.

Action-learning

Many young people leave school and join the Youth Training Scheme. It is important to know what you are joining, and what kind of training you will get.

The best way to find out about the Youth Training Scheme is to go and visit a scheme – and to ask the trainees themselves about it.

Use the questionnaire on page 23 to help you find out what the scheme is like.

YTS Questionnaire

See page 24 for instructions.

1 What is the name of your YTS scheme? _____

2 What kind of scheme is it?

[ ] (a) Mode A, employer-based

[ ] (b) Mode B1, Community Project

[ ] (c) Mode B1, Training Workshop

[ ] (d) Mode B1, Information Technology Centre (ITEC)

[ ] (e) Mode B2, College-based scheme, with work-experience

3 How long have you been on it? _____

4 Are you on a one-year scheme or a two-year scheme? _____

5 How much are you getting paid each week? _____

6 What are you doing today on the scheme? _____

7 Can you tell me three practical things that you are learning on the scheme at the moment?
(a) _____
(b) _____
(c) _____

8 What are the main skills which you will develop during this year? _____

9 How much time do you spend in classroom training sessions? _____ per week/month

10 What new tools or equipment are you learning to use?
(a)   (b)   (c)

11 How do the staff or supervisors closest to you treat you? Please mark a score, 0–10:
(a) Friendly, as equals   10 9 8 7 6 5 4 3 2 1 0   Distant, as children
(b) They help us to learn   10 9 8 7 6 5 4 3 2 1 0   They order us about

12 How do the male staff/supervisors treat the young women trainees on the scheme?
As complete equals   10 9 8 7 6 5 4 3 2 1 0   They don't take us/them seriously

13 How do the white staff/supervisors treat black, Asian and other ethnic-minority trainees on the scheme?
As complete equals   10 9 8 7 6 5 4 3 2 1 0   They look down on us/them

14 Have you been away on a residential course while on the scheme? Yes/no/going soon

15 If you have, where did you go? _____

16 If you have, how did you find the course?
(a) Lots of fun   10 9 8 7 6 5 4 3 2 1 0   No fun at all
(b) I learned a lot   10 9 8 7 6 5 4 3 2 1 0   I didn't learn anything new at all
(c) Very challenging   10 9 8 7 6 5 4 3 2 1 0   Not challenging at all

17 What percentage of trainees on your scheme last year went into jobs within three weeks of leaving the scheme?   100 90 80 70 60 50 40 30 20 10 0%

18 Are you given help to find a job while on the scheme? _____

19 What happens if someone misbehaves while on the scheme? _____

20 What happens if you are late for work in the morning? _____

21 Are you encouraged to make suggestions about possible changes to the scheme? _____

22 Do you consider that you are being used as cheap labour, or are you definitely receiving a training?
Real training   10 9 8 7 6 5 4 3 2 1 0   Cheap labour

23 Does your scheme take proper measures to protect your health and safety?
Yes, excellent   10 9 8 7 6 5 4 3 2 1 0   No, very poor

24 Have you been asked if you want to join a trade union?
Yes/No   Have you joined one? Yes/No   Which? _____

25 How pleased are you that you joined the scheme?
Very pleased   10 9 8 7 6 5 4 3 2 1 0   Not pleased at all

26 What are your main difficulties on the scheme?
(a) _____
(b) _____
(c) _____

27 What changes would you make to the scheme? _____

28 Finally, would you recommend the scheme to other young people? _____
Very strongly   10 9 8 7 6 5 4 3 2 1 0   Not at all _____

YTS Action-learning

Action-learning 1: building up a scoring system

Purpose: To build up a profile of YTS schemes in the locality, as seen by the trainees.

1 Two or three people visit the Careers Service, and collect full information about the Youth Training Scheme, and the addresses of all the major firms and groups which are participating in the locality.

2 Obtain permission to visit one scheme, *taking the questionnaire with you*. Interview five to ten trainees.

3 Discuss your results.

4 Decide together what are the important features of a YTS scheme which should be scored, and work out a point scoring system.

5 Make changes to the questionnaire, dropping questions, adding new questions or changing the wording of existing questions, so that it covers everything that you want to know.

6 Visit another YTS scheme with the improved questionnaire. This time, invite trainees to fill it in on their own, without any assistance, except where a question is not clear.

7 Discuss your results, and make any final changes to the questionnaire, so that trainees can fill it in on their own.

8 Make arrangements with the Area Board of the Manpower Services Commission (MSC) for you to carry out a survey of trainees in local schemes. Contact them through the Careers Service.

9 Working singly or in pairs, deliver the questionnaires to trainees, and bring them back completed.

10 Add up the scores from the trainees on each scheme, so that you obtain an overall score for each scheme.

11 You now have a choice over what to do with your results. You could:
   ● Hold a press conference, and release your results to the press locally
   ● Keep them private, for use by students who are making decisions about joining YTS
   ● Contact radio or TV stations, and organise a public discussion about your results.

12 If (by any chance) someone tells you not to ask trainees to fill in the questionnaire, you can:
   (a) Get advice from the MSC Area Board's Trade Union representative, careers officers and local councillors
   (b) Write letters to the press
   (c) Ask scheme organisers individually whether they have any objections
   (d) Proceed anyway, asking trainees to fill in the questionnaire in their lunch hour or after working hours.

If you meet objections, from the MSC or employers, it may be (a) because they don't like some of the questions, in which case you could change the wording, or (b) because they don't want to risk obtaining a low score for their scheme. If you need support, write to: The Director, Youth Aid, 9 Poland St, London W1.

Action-learning 2: visits

Visit YTS schemes, and invite some trainees to come to the school and talk about what it is like being a trainee. Permission for this should be obtained from their training supervisors. You are almost certain to find them very co-operative. Ask the trainees to take some photographic slides of their scheme and of the other trainees, and to bring them with them, to make their talk more interesting.

Action-learning 3: skills chart

Obtain the addresses of all the local YTS schemes from the Careers Service, and visit each scheme to find out what practical and general skills the trainees are learning.

Then create a massive wall-chart, listing all of these skills along the top, and the names of the schemes down the side, marking which skills which can be learned on each scheme on the chart.

This will enable anyone wanting to learn, eg, painting and decorating, or book-keeping, to see at once which schemes teach this skill.

The Community Programme

Fancy a job on the Community Programme?

The Community Programme provides both full-time and part-time jobs:

● for young people aged between 18 and 24 who have been out of work for at least six out of the last nine months

● and for adults who have been out of work for over a year.

The jobs which it provides also offer you a chance to help your local community, in a wide variety of projects:

Clearing derelict canals
Running adventure playgrounds
Renovating buildings
Gardening for elderly people

Planting trees
Running city farms
Insulating lofts
Special tourism projects

and a hundred other projects, set up by local people in an attempt to create jobs and do something useful at the same time. The projects are organised by Managing Agencies, and financed by the Manpower Services Commission (MSC). There are about 300,000 people on Community Programme projects in Britain.

Action-learning

● Visit the Jobcentre, and bring back a full listing of all the local Community Programme projects, and a description of what each one offers.

● If the description is not detailed enough, phone up each project, and ask them to send you full details, including a clear list of the skills which CP workers will develop.

● Create a skills list, which shows clearly what skills you will learn while on a CP project, so that you are better able to choose which one interests you.

● Use the questionnaire opposite, or a developed version of it, and visit CP projects to interview workers, to find out what they think about the programme.

● Find out what percentage of workers on each CP project go on to full-time jobs or training when they leave the Community Programme.

● Develop a scoring system for each project, and for each Managing Agency, in order to see which are good and which are not so good projects. Publish the results.

Community Programme questionnaire

1 What is the name of this project? _____

2 How long have you been on it? _____

3 What are the main types of work that you are doing?
_____
_____
_____

4 (a) How much do you get paid per week?
(b) Do you receive any additional income, in Family Benefit or Housing Benefit?

5 Are you learning any new skills? Yes ☐ No ☐
(a) Which skills? _____
_____
_____

6 How pleased are you to be on the project?
Very pleased   Not pleased
10 9 8 7 6 5 4 3 2 1 0

7 Do you know what percentage of workers on the project are going on to full-time jobs or training when they finish?
90% 80 70 60 50
40 30 20 10%

8 Are you satisfied with the assistance you are given to help you find a job when you leave the project?
Very satisfied   Not satisfied at all
10 9 8 7 6 5 4 3 2 1 0
(a) What kind of assistance are you given?
_____

9 Has your personal confidence increased or fallen while you have been on the project?
Increased
+10 +9 +8 +7 +6 +5 +4 +3 +2 +1 0
Fallen
−1 −2 −3 −4 −5 −6 −7 −8 −9 −10

10 What changes would you like to see made to the project?
(a) _____
(b) _____
(c) _____

Full-time training and education

Fancy going to college or training full-time?

Statements about college

1 'Education is for educated people.' Agree/disagree

2 'College is just like school.' Agree/disagree

3 'My parents never went to college, so they don't give me much encouragement to do so.' True/untrue/partly true

4 'It's not a proper job.' Agree/disagree

5 'Going to college can really help you to get some useful qualifications.' Agree/disagree

Questions

1 How much do you know about the local colleges?

Lots   Nothing at all
10 9 8 7 6 5 4 3 2 1 0

2 Are you interested in finding out more about what kind of courses you can study at college?

Very interested   Not interested at all
10 9 8 7 6 5 4 3 2 1 0

3 Which of the following practical training courses do you think can be studied in colleges (tick where 'yes')

- [ ] Hairdressing
- [ ] Electronics
- [ ] Horticulture
- [ ] Business skills
- [ ] Secretarial skills
- [ ] Bricklaying
- [ ] Television repair
- [ ] Art and sculpture
- [ ] Office management
- [ ] Painting and decorating
- [ ] Printing
- [ ] Fabric design

- [ ] Car mechanics
- [ ] Computing
- [ ] Catering
- [ ] Accountancy
- [ ] Banking
- [ ] Carpentry
- [ ] Design skills
- [ ] Dance
- [ ] Textiles
- [ ] Word processing
- [ ] Hotel management
- [ ] Furniture restoration

(For answers see page 47)

4 Did you know that many MSC training courses, for which you can receive a training allowance, are run at colleges? Yes/no

5 Do you know what kind of MSC training courses are available? Yes/no/not really

6 Where should you go to find out about MSC training courses? (a) The Jobcentre (b) The local college (c) The library (d) The local council (e) The Citizens Advice Bureau (See page 47)

7 Which of these reasons **for** taking up a course at a college do you agree with? Give each reason a score from 0 to 10 (10 = fully agree, 0 = not a good reason). Score 0–10:
(a) ____ I will be able to pass some exams
(b) ____ I will be able to learn some valuable new skills
(c) ____ It will help me to get a good job, when I finish
(d) ____ I will make some good friends, and have a good time
(e) ____ I will learn more about the world in general
——
     Total score
——

8 Which of these reasons **against** taking up a course at a college do you agree with? Again, give each reason a score, from 0 to 10.
(a) ____ I am not good enough to do a course
(b) ____ It won't pay me any proper money
(c) ____ None of my friends have gone to college
(d) ____ I don't understand what college is all about
(e) ____ I'm fed up with sitting in classrooms
——
     Total score
——

Action-learning

● Arrange a visit to the college, and a meeting with a tutor who can explain how it all works.

● Invite two or three students at the college to come in and talk about the college, and what it is like.

● Get details of all the different classes that are available, and play 'IMAGINE', imagining you could join any classes, without having to worry about anything, like money, friends or uncertainties. Create a big list on the wall of all the courses which you could join. Arrange a meeting to find out about applying for courses which interest you.

● Create a questionnaire similar to the one on page 23 to obtain student opinions about college life.

Note:

You can also attend college part time, and join whatever classes you like. If you are unemployed and receiving benefit, you can attend classes for up to 21 hours a week.

Active unemployment

What is your 'positive unemployment' score?

Which of the following do you think you would do, if you were unemployed? (Tick where 'yes')

A

☐ Get up early most days

☐ Take up a sport

☐ Get regular exercise twice a week (or more)

☐ Get involved in community activities

☐ Start hitchhiking, in order to get around

☐ Get hold of a bicycle, somehow

☐ Start reading some interesting books

☐ Join a local club in a hobby that interests me

☐ Join a local voluntary action group

☐ Find ways to earn small amounts of money (legally – £4 per week)

☐ Try to form a small odd jobs co-operative, as an alternative to the dole

☐ Think seriously about starting my own business

☐ Start using the local library to find good books to read

☐ Visit the nearest unemployed centre, to find out what is happening there

☐ Spend some time every day looking for work

☐ Spend some time every week looking for work

☐ Ask someone to help me with my application letters

☐ Buy the local paper every day, to look for jobs

☐ Tell all my friends that I am looking for work, in case they can help me

☐ Visit the careers office and the Jobcentre regularly, to ask about work

☐ Get together with some friends to do something positive together

☐ Get hold of a good book about unemployment, and learn how to use my time wisely

☐ Offer to do all the cooking and shopping on at least one day a week

☐ Visit the local college to find out about daytime or evening classes

☐ Take up a daytime or evening class

☐ Start learning some new skills

☐ Start learning how to speak a foreign language

☐ Go out walking, hiking or cycling with friends

☐ Have a lot of fun, and do crazy things with friends

☐ Try to keep up a positive attitude of mind, whatever happens

___ Total A (number of ticks)

Or would you: **B**

☐ Hang around the streets with my friends, doing nothing much

☐ Stay up late every night watching TV

☐ Rent videos, and spend the nights watching them with my friends

☐ Mess around with drugs

☐ Grow gradually more depressed and fed up

☐ Gradually stop bothering about looking for work

☐ Find myself gradually getting more negative, both about life and about myself?

(each item scores 4 points)

___ Total B

Positive unemployment score: Total A – Total B = ————

Opinions

1 Unemployed people are generally lazy. They could all find jobs if they really wanted to. Agree/disagree

2 Unemployment in Britain is caused by:
   (a) government policies. Yes/no/maybe
   (b) trade unions demanding too high wages. Yes/no/maybe
   (c) modern technologies – robots, computers, etc. Yes/no/maybe
   (d) the decline of the industrial age. Yes/no/maybe
   (e) international competition – imports from countries such as Japan. Yes/no/maybe
   (f) an increase in the number of people wanting to work. Yes/no/maybe
   (g) regional problems and inequalities within Britain. Yes/no/maybe
   (h) a mixture of different factors. Yes/no/maybe
   (Answers, see page 47)

3 Unemployment can offer a real opportunity to people to start exploring their own lives, and doing something positive. Agree/disagree

● Do you think that school prepares people for possible unemployment in a positive way? Yes/no

● Do you think that it is possible to adopt a positive attitude when you are unemployed? Yes/no

● Do you think that it makes a difference whether you adopt a positive or a negative attitude, when you are unemployed? Yes/no

A period of unemployment can be a positive time. You can learn new things, meet new people, develop new skills, and use the time to explore your life. You have a **choice** whether to adopt a negative or a positive attitude. These pages have been written to encourage a positive attitude.

● How much do you enjoy your school life (training scheme, current work)? Rate it on a scale of 0 to 100 on line A, 0 = Do not enjoy it, 100 = Enjoy it completely.

● How much do you enjoy your leisure? Rate it in a similar way on line B.

A   0   10   20   30   40   50   60   70   80   90   100

B   0   10   20   30   40   50   60   70   80   90   100

Draw a thick double line linking your two scores. Then ask the other people in your group to call out their scores, and draw in single lines for them in the same way. Do you notice anything about the lines?

Why do you think people find being unemployed so difficult to take?

☐ Shortage of money

☐ Boredom

☐ Having no friends from work

☐ Having fears about the future

☐ Becoming depressed and gloomy

☐ Feeling that you are useless and worthless

☐ Being ashamed to tell people about it, or to talk about it

☐ Drifting around, doing nothing

☐ Having no sense of direction

How do you use your leisure time?

Think back over the last week, and write down what you did each evening, and at the weekend in the spaces below. When you have done that, give each one a score, from 0 to 10:

10 A really good time
8 A good time
6 Quite a good time

4 Not bad, I suppose
2 Not much fun, really
0 Boring. Waste of time

What I did	Score
Monday evening	☐
Tuesday evening	☐
Wednesday evening	☐
Thursday evening	☐
Friday evening	☐
Saturday morning	☐
Saturday afternoon	☐
Saturday evening	☐
Sunday am/pm	☐
Sunday evening	☐
Total leisure score:	—

If you were unemployed, what kind of things would you like to achieve over the next three months?

You may feel 'I don't know where to begin'. Don't worry. Once you begin to think about it and talk about it with your friends, you will begin to get ideas. The ideas presented in this book may help you.

What kind of thing would you like to achieve, over the next three months?

☐ Learn a new skill

☐ Practise a skill I've already got

☐ Spend some time playing sports and keeping fit

☐ Explore – go to places I've not been to before

☐ Meet some new people

☐ Earn some money, on top of my benefit

☐ Have a go at going self-employed (or setting up a co-operative) and earning my own living

☐ Become involved in a national or local campaign on an issue that I feel strongly about

☐ Spend time reading, making music, painting, making things, dancing. Which?

☐ Enjoy myself

☐ _____

Setting goals

Linda, aged 18, is unemployed. But she wants to be **actively** unemployed.

In order to help herself to meet her goals, she has drawn up the following **goal chart**.

If you have plans of your own that you want to achieve, add them to the list. Think about the list, and choose your 'top ten', numbering them from 1 to 10.

Goal	Notes and ideas	Actions I can take next week
1 Regular jobhunting	Join a Jobclub at the Jobcentre? Get a good book on jobhunting from the library. Visit the library every day to scan through the local papers.	Visit the Jobcentre on **Tuesday morning**. Go to the library **every evening around 5.30**, when the papers come out. Ask the librarian about a good book on jobhunting.
2 Do something voluntary with children	Are there any local playgroups? I'd like to find out about training courses, too. Visit the Careers Service?	Visit the Careers Service on **Monday morning**, to ask about training involving children. Ask them how I can find out about voluntary work in a local playgroup, too.
3 Take up a sport, to keep fit and healthy	Don't know what to do. Visit the sports centre to find out what is available. Talk to my friend Karen, to see if she's got any ideas. Fancy karate, but I'm afraid it'll be all blokes there.	Get Karen to come with me to the sports centre – **Thursday afternoon**? Find out about karate at the same time.
4 Join a local group which is doing something to help the environment	Don't know where to begin here. Might ask at the library. Is there a Friends of the Earth group locally?	Ask at the library about groups. Spend time **Monday morning** looking around town for notices about any local groups or meetings.
5 Start learning about computers	Don't know where to begin here either. Could try asking at the Careers Service or the Jobcentre.	Ask at the Jobcentre on **Tuesday morning.** Ask at the Careers Service, too.
6 Take up an evening class in dressmaking	Visit the local Community Centre, and ask them what I should do.	Visit the Community Centre on **Wednesday morning** to ask about classes. May need to visit the local college, too – **Friday morning**?

These plans begin to form Linda's diary for the week ahead, which appears at the top of the next page.

Every goal can lead to an action of some sort – either a direct action, or asking someone about action, or asking someone to find out who you should ask.
There is never a goal that leads to no action.

A weekly diary

Linda's diary: Week one

	Morning	Afternoon	Evening
Monday	Visit the Careers Service. Look around town for notices about local groups	5.30 visit library	Write any job applications
Tuesday	Visit Jobcentre, ask about Jobclub, also computer courses	5.30 library	Application letters
Wednesday	Visit Community Centre, ask about dressmaking class	5.30 library	Evening with friends
Thursday		Visit Sports Centre with Karen. Ask about activities, and about karate. 5.30 library	
Friday	Visit college, ask about computers and dressmaking classes	5.30 library	Application letters

Now look back to the action plan on page 20. You can make your own goals chart and action plan. As your first actions lead to other actions, you will begin to reach your goals.

One large goal is reached by many small steps.

'I am interested to learn about photography'

has to become

'I will visit the library to see if there are any evening classes I could attend, and if there is a photographic society that I could join'

'Those voluntary work camps sound interesting'

has to become

'I will write to the address mentioned (p 40) to find out more details'

and

'I would like a chance to go canoeing'

has to become

'I will telephone the Youth Office and arrange a time when I can go in and meet someone to talk about the possibility.'

Quality job-hunting — a checklist

- [ ] 1 Have you written yourself a 'Personal Information Chart'?

- [ ] 2 Have you had copies made of it?

- [ ] 3 Do you have a notebook or file, where you keep a record of your jobhunting efforts?

- [ ] 4 Are you calling at the Careers Office and Jobcentre regularly, or phoning if you cannot call?

- [ ] 5 Have you registered with any local employment agencies?

- [ ] 6 Do you keep a daily check on jobs in the daily papers?

- [ ] 7 Do you keep a weekly check on jobs in the weekly papers?

- [ ] 8 Do you keep a check on jobs in any relevant magazines?

- [ ] 9 Are you writing letters 'on spec' to possible employers?

- [ ] 10 Are you making visits 'on spec' to possible employers, on an organised basis, taking your Personal Information Chart?

- [ ] 11 Have you told your friends and neighbours that you are looking for work, so that they can keep their eyes open for you?

- [ ] 12 Are you making new friends and meeting new people, by becoming involved in new activities? The more friends you have, the wider will be your personal 'grapevine'

- [ ] 13 Do you check local notice boards each week?

- [ ] 14 Do you feel that you write a good application letter?

- [ ] 15 Do you feel that you always fill in application forms in the best way?

- [ ] 16 Do you feel confident about your interview manner?

- [ ] 17 Do you prepare carefully for an interview, by finding out about the job, thinking of questions to ask, etc?

- [ ] 18 Have you ever had any dummy interview practice?

- [ ] 19 Do you feel confident about your manner on the telephone?

- [ ] 20 Have you applied to join a Job Club?

- [ ] **Total Score**

Scoring:
14–20: You are doing well in your jobhunting efforts. It may be useful to check on the points you did not score on, in order to improve still further.

7–13: You are doing quite well – probably as well as anyone else. There is still a lot more that you could be doing, however.

0–6: You have good reason to feel hopeful, because there is a lot of room for improvement in your jobhunting, which might bring you success.

Action-learning

● Borrow a video-camera, and practise dummy job interviews. Then invite a local business person to come in and interview people, to help you learn what it is like.

● Working in pairs, make appointments to interview different local employers, to find out what kind of qualities they are looking for in young people. Write their answers down, and bring your results back to share with the group.

● Choose people to go along to the local Jobclub for a day, at the Jobcentre (if there is one), to find out what the members of the club do, and what they think of it.

(This exercise has been taken from *The New Unemployment Handbook*, with permission from the National Extension College.)

Further reading
There are many good books on job-hunting on the market, which you can use to improve your quality. *The New Unemployment Handbook* (NEC) is one; *My Job Application File* and *Your First Move* (both CRAC books) are others.

Earning small amounts of money

Opinions

'It is illegal for unemployed people to earn anything extra on top of their dole.' True/false
'If YTS trainees earn extra money in their spare time, it is taken off their training allowances.' True/false
'College students can earn extra money, but their grants will be reduced if they do.' True/false
'Most young people could easily earn a bit of extra money, if they put their minds to it.' Agree/disagree

The facts

● If you are at school, on the YTS scheme, at college, or on the Community Programme, you can earn as much money as you want to in your spare time, without your grants or allowances being affected.

● Unemployed people can also earn a little extra money each week, under the following rules.

The rules

The 1987 DHSS rule about earning money while you are unemployed is as follows: you may earn up to £4 a week, **after expenses**, before your benefit is affected. If you earn more than that, your benefit will be reduced by exactly the amount which you earn.

In 1988, this rule will change, allowing unemployed people to earn £5 a week, with no allowance for expenses.

In Glastonbury, a group of unemployed people met together one or two days a week, assisted by a local woman. They went out and did odd jobs – gardening, clearing rubble, painting, etc. From the money which they earned, they kept £4 each (which was allowed under the DHSS rules). They put the rest into a group bank account, and used it to pay for their expenses. These included buying rainproof jackets and boots, buying gardening equipment, and taking driving lessons.

Action-learning

● Do a group brainstorm* on different ways in which you could earn extra money. Go on creating ideas (legal and illegal, funny and serious) until you have 35 different ideas. Then pick out 15 ideas which you could do next week.

● Break up into small groups of two or three. During the next week, you are to choose a way to earn extra money, and actually earn it. Next week, you will be given a chance to tell the others how you did it.

● Visit the local DHSS office, and find out exactly what are the rules about unemployed people earning money. Then create a poster explaining it, and display it in a shop window, or in a Community Centre window.

● Create a simple questionnaire asking people if they know whether unemployed people are allowed to earn money, and if so, what the rules are. Go out on to the streets, and find ten people each to interview. Then come back, and share your results.

* Brainstorms

A brainstorm is a way in which a group of people can produce a big list of ideas in a short space of time.
Warm-up: Ask your group to break up into small groups of three or four people. Ask each group to think up **as many uses as possible** for, eg, one old boot (ask for a sample from the group), and write them down.

Rules: The rules of a good brainstorm are very simple:
1 Every idea suggested is written down by a volunteer in the group.
2 Work quickly, and think up ideas as quickly as you can.
3 The ideas that people suggest are not discussed or criticised at all.
4 Silly, funny, illegal and immoral ideas are all equally welcome, as well as sensible, practical ideas. Laughter encourages the flow of ideas.
5 A time limit is set in advance, eg three or five minutes.

When the groups have created their lists of ideas, ask each small group to choose their favourite three ideas, one humorous or silly idea and two serious, practical ideas. Then each group shares these with the rest of the group. Then try a second warm-up (eg 'as many ways as you can think of to improve school/YTS/college meals' **or** 'as many ways as you can think of to start up a relationship with a man/woman' **or** 'as many ways as you can think of to improve the DHSS office/improve the school common room/develop a better relationship with your boss/supervisor/teacher'). Then brainstorm on the subject you need results on, ie ways in which you can earn extra money.

Budgeting

What is your present weekly income? _____

How do you spend it? In the far left-hand column below, make a list of everything that you spend money on, leaving few blanks at the bottom for things you think of later. Keep track of all your expenditure this week, day by day, entering the amount you spend each day in the correct column:

	Mon	Tues	Wed	Thur	Fri	Sat	Sun
Payment to parents	_____	_____	_____	_____	_____	_____	_____
Food	_____	_____	_____	_____	_____	_____	_____
Papers and magazines	_____	_____	_____	_____	_____	_____	_____
Clothes, shoes	_____	_____	_____	_____	_____	_____	_____
Stationery, books	_____	_____	_____	_____	_____	_____	_____
Make-up, chemist's supplies	_____	_____	_____	_____	_____	_____	_____
Bus/train fares	_____	_____	_____	_____	_____	_____	_____
Records, cassettes	_____	_____	_____	_____	_____	_____	_____
Cigarettes	_____	_____	_____	_____	_____	_____	_____
Drinks	_____	_____	_____	_____	_____	_____	_____
Cinema, disco	_____	_____	_____	_____	_____	_____	_____
Savings scheme	_____	_____	_____	_____	_____	_____	_____
Rent	_____	_____	_____	_____	_____	_____	_____
Tools, equipment	_____	_____	_____	_____	_____	_____	_____
Stamps	_____	_____	_____	_____	_____	_____	_____
Phone calls	_____	_____	_____	_____	_____	_____	_____
Petrol	_____	_____	_____	_____	_____	_____	_____
Coke, sweets, ice cream, etc	_____	_____	_____	_____	_____	_____	_____
_____	_____	_____	_____	_____	_____	_____	_____
_____	_____	_____	_____	_____	_____	_____	_____

Totals: _____ + _____ + _____ + _____ + _____ + _____ + _____

Week's total income: _____ **Fortnightly income:** _____
Weekly total expenditure: _____ **Fortnightly expenditure:** _____
Surplus (+) or deficit (−): _____ **Surplus/deficit:** _____

Making your money go further

● If you were able to save £200, what would you do with it? Divide up the money as you would use it, in column A:

A	
_____	Put it in a bank deposit account
_____	Take a holiday
_____	Buy mum/dad a big gift
_____	_____
_____	_____
_____	_____
_____	_____
£200	**Total**

How could you manage to get hold of £200?

1 I could open a **savings account**, and put something into it every week (how much? £ _____)

2 I could buy a **piggy bank**, and save 50p/20p pieces. (Guess at my weekly savings: possibly £ _____ per week)

3 Looking at my list of weekly expenditure, I could **cut back** my expenditure on
(a) _____ (saving £ _____ per week)
(b) _____ (saving £ _____ per week)
(c) _____ (saving £ _____ per week)

4 I could **earn extra money** by _____ or by _____ In this way, I could earn £ _____ per week.

5 I could **sell** my _____   Method of sale
(a) _____ (sale value £ _____)   _____
(b) _____ (sale value £ _____)   _____
(c) _____ (sale value £ _____)   _____

(Methods of sale: to friends, on a market stall, through the newspaper, through a card in a shop window, _____)

6 I could **gamble** £ _____ each week at the horses (_____), bingo (_____), football pools (_____), playing cards (_____), and hope to win £ _____ or to lose £ _____ I reckon my chances of winning are (underline):
20 to 1   2 to 1   Even   1 in 2   1 in 20   1 in 50   1 in 100   1 in 1000

7 I could **borrow** £ _____ from _____ , repaying it by money gained by method
1 / 2 / 3/ 4 / 5 above (circle which), within _____ weeks/months.

Total money acquired in a lump sum (by a sale or loan) = £ _____
Total money acquired on a weekly basis (saving or earning) = £ _____
Total money saved or earned over 10 weeks = £ _____

How long will it take you to build up £200? _____

Supplementary benefit/income support

It is expected that the whole system of supplementary benefit will change, and become 'income support' during the life of this book. No precise details about these systems are therefore being printed. Instead, an action-learning approach is recommended.

Action-learning

● Try to find answers to these questions:
1 What kind of basic benefit can young unemployed people receive, and on what conditions?
2 What provision can be made to cover the costs of housing, rent, etc?
3 What provision can be made to cover the cost of board and lodging in a hostel, and on what conditions?
4 How much extra money are unemployed people allowed to earn on top of their benefit?
5 How do people apply to receive benefit?
6 What should you do if you think you are not getting the right benefit, or if you want to complain?
7 Who can assist unemployed people to get the benefit they are entitled to?

● Divide your group up into four subgroups to find answers to the questions.
Group A goes to the local office of the Department of Health and Social Security (DHSS).
Group B goes to the local Citizens Advice Bureau.

Group C goes either to a Centre for Unemployed People, a Community Centre, a local Resource Centre or a Housing Advice Centre.
Group D goes out onto the streets and interviews people, asking individual people for their answers to the same questions.

Groups A–C, while finding the answers to their questions, might give the group they interview two scores, from 0 to 10, showing (a) how friendly and (b) how useful they were.

animals
archaeology
astrology
astronomy
badminton
ballet
batik
beauty care
beer-making
billiards
boxing
braille
building
campaigning
camping
canoeing
caving
chess
children
climbing
computers
cookery
cricket
cycling
dancing
designing
disco-dance
discussions
diving
DIY skills
drama
drawing
dress design
driving
ecology
electronics
fencing
film-making
first aid
fishing
folk music
French
gardening
German
golf
guitar
gymnastics
hi-fi
hiking
ice-skating
Italian
jewellery
jogging
judo
karate
knitting
leatherwork
life-saving
marriage
metalwork
miming
model-making
money
motorbikes
motor cars
murals
music-making
mythology
nature
navigation
netball
new ideas
painting
peace movement
photography
piano
poetry
politics
pottery
punting
puppetry
reading
religion
riding
rugby
rock bands
sailing
sculpture
shorthand
slimnastics
shooting
singing
spinning
squash
sub aqua
swimming
table tennis
talking to people
tennis
topography
typing
weaving
Welsh
wine-making
woodcarving
woodwork
work with the handicapped
world affairs
writing
yoga

What interests you?

● Look at this list, and make a tick by each activity that interests you. Add any extra interests in the spaces provided.
● Then go around the list again, and place stars opposite the 15 activities which interest you the most.
● Now pick out your **top five interests**, and write them in the spaces below.

1 _____

2 _____

3 _____

4 _____

5 _____

35

Learning new skills

Which of the following do you think are possible for people who are unemployed?

	Yes	No
1 Going to college on a part-time basis	☐	☐
2 Studying for an Open University course or degree	☐	☐
3 Learning how to do car repair and maintenance	☐	☐
4 Doing a children's playgroup course	☐	☐
5 Doing a full-time college course	☐	☐
6 Learning karate, judo, yoga, tai chi or taikwondo	☐	☐
7 Learning Russian, Spanish or French	☐	☐
8 Learning to be a group leader	☐	☐
9 Learning how to organise a petition to present to an MP	☐	☐
10 Learning how to work as a team	☐	☐
11 Learning how to drive	☐	☐
12 Learning how to cope with difficulties	☐	☐
13 Learning how to take control over your own life	☐	☐
14 Learning how to chair a meeting	☐	☐
15 Taking biology, mathematics or sociology GSCE	☐	☐
16 Taking a metalwork or electronics City and Guilds exam	☐	☐
17 Learning how to produce a magazine	☐	☐
18 Learning how to be a potter	☐	☐
19 Learning how to operate a computer or word processor	☐	☐
20 Learning to be a carpenter	☐	☐

(For answers see page 47)

'Skills' does not just mean practical-skills

There are at least four different types of skill – see the four boxes. How good do you think you are at each of the skills listed? (In box A, you must first fill in your own skills.) Give yourself a star-rating from 0 to 5 in the spaces after each skill.

Personal skills   0–5

Talking ☐

Listening ☐

Self-organisation ☐

Relationships ☐

Initiative ☐

Survival skills   0–5

How to tackle problems/where to go for help ☐

How to complain or appeal ☐

Cheap living/saving money ☐

Expressing your feelings ☐

Picking yourself up when you're down ☐

Practical skills

Skills you've already got:
                                                            0–5
1 ☐

2 ☐

3 ☐

Skills you want to improve:

4 ☐

5 ☐

Organisational skills   0–5

Working as a group/team ☐

Making decisions ☐

Tackling obstacles ☐

Getting work done to schedule ☐

Taking the lead ☐

What is your total score? _____

(maximum 100)

Developing your own skills

● Make a list of five skills you would like to develop:

_____
_____
_____
_____
_____

● Copy your five top interests from page 35:

_____
_____
_____
_____
_____

Now decide how you could learn or develop
(a) each of these five skills, and (b) each of your five interests from page 35.

Ways of learning

There are nine major ways of learning. Write the name of each skill or interest you want to learn or develop opposite the way (or ways) you think you will best learn it:

1 By going to the local college for up to
   21 hours a week   _____
2 By studying at evening class   _____
3 By either staying at school or returning to
   school   _____
4 By learning direct from somebody you
   ask, either a friend, a relative or someone local   _____
5 By joining a Skills Sharing Network if
   there is one locally   _____
6 By personal practice and learning
7 By study from books, cassettes,
   radio and TV, etc   _____
8 By taking part in local groups, clubs and
   activities   _____
9 By living your life as actively as you can   _____

Opinion: It is very difficult for people who are unemployed to learn new skills. True/false

Community activity

In every village, town and city there are groups of people who are working together at voluntary community activities.

● Place a tick after each of the community activities listed below which you think you would enjoy doing.

● Then give a score from 1 to 5 to the ones you have ticked. you have ticked.
(1 = Quite interested, 5 = Very interested).

☐ Helping to clear out an old canal _____

☐ Putting on a disco as a fundraiser for a community group _____

☐ Doing a sponsored bed-push around the town, to raise funds _____

☐ Working with a local Oxfam, Greenpeace or Friends of the Earth group, to help make the world a better place _____

☐ Helping to organise a summer playscheme for children with a physical handicap _____

☐ Taking old people out on shopping expeditions _____

☐ Helping to build an adventure playground _____

☐ Joining a group which is planting trees, to make the area more beautiful _____

☐ Helping to run an advice centre for other young people _____

☐ Working to open up a permanent centre where young people could meet to form bands and play music _____

☐ Joining a drama group, and doing musical dramas, street theatre, puppetry, mime, children's theatre, etc together _____

☐ Joining a local writers' group, and creating a book about local history by interviewing old people _____

☐ Helping to make a video about something of local interest _____

☐ Creating and painting an exciting mural, with other people _____

☐ Putting on an exhibition of paintings, sculptures, poems, writings and drawings by young unemployed people _____

☐ Getting together with other people and creating your own weekly radio show for young people _____

☐ Helping to run a club for mentally handicapped people _____

☐ Making bird boxes and bat boxes, with other people, to help encourage bird life _____

☐ Doing a survey of local plant-life and butterfly life in a local park _____

☐ Helping to run a centre for unemployed people, as a volunteer _____

1 Where would you go to find out what is happening locally, and how you could join in? In the list below, place a tick in column A by each place where you think you might be able to find out what is happening.

2 Then place a tick in column B if you know how to find it.

A B

☐ ☐ The local library

☐ ☐ The police station

☐ ☐ The Citizens Advice Bureau

☐ ☐ A youth club

☐ ☐ A community centre

☐ ☐ A centre for unemployed people

☐ ☐ A local 'Council for Voluntary Service' or volunteer bureau

☐ ☐ The Youth Service

☐ ☐ The Careers Service

☐ ☐ The Community or Adult Education Centre

☐ ☐ The Post Office

☐ ☐ The local college

☐ ☐ Looking for posters and notices in shop windows

☐ ☐ Looking for notices in the local paper

☐ ☐ A local community magazine

☐ ☐

Action-learning
● Divide up the list of places where you might be able to find out what is happening, and go out in small groups of two or three and gather up as much practical information about groups, meetings and activities as you can. Then display it all in different sections (sports, children, nature conservation, etc) on a wall, or somewhere where everyone can see it.

Joining together as a group
In many towns and cities, young people have joined together to form groups to do things together. Imagine that you were unemployed (or perhaps you are). Which of the activities listed below appeals to you? Give each activity a score from 0 to 10 (0 = No appeal at all, 10 = lots of appeal):

0–10

_____ Arranging to get together to earn £4 each a week by doing odd jobs. (£4 is the legal weekly earning limit for unemployed people – see p 32)

_____ Setting up a small youth co-operative, to earn enough money to sign off the dole altogether

_____ Setting up a seven-a-side football team, or a swimming/tennis/badminton (etc) team, and challenging other local youth teams (or the DHSS)

_____ Going camping together for a weekend

_____ Arranging a canoeing or mountaineering expedition together, with help from the Youth Office

_____ Putting on a disco, to raise funds

_____ Forming a rock band, dance group or theatre group

_____ Producing your own young people's magazine

_____ Raising the money to hire a minibus, and then going away for a holiday together

_____ Helping each other with jobhunting, and with writing application letters

_____ Doing crazy things together, like having a midnight feast out in the country

_____ Going away on a voluntary work camp or a nature conservation camp together (see p 40)

_____ Going to the sports centre together, to do weightlifting, aerobics, gymnastics, trampolining, etc

_____ Helping each other with personal and family matters, as they come up

_____ Just helping each other, and spending time together

Group difficulties
What do you think would be the biggest difficulties you would run into, if you were to set up a young people's group together? Add your own ideas, and then give each difficulty a score, from 0 to 10 (0 = Not a difficulty, 10 = Very big difficulty):

_____ Not being able to come to any agreements together

_____ Not having good ideas

_____ Not having proper information about things that we could do

_____ Arguing

_____ Not following up on things that we agreed to do

_____ Not having the confidence to do new things

_____ Not having the money to do things

_____ _____

Action-learning
● Find out if there is a young people's group meeting locally. (Ask at the Youth Service, a community centre, the centre for unemployed people, etc). Talk with them, and find out how they got set up, what they do, what their hopes are, and what difficulties they have run into. Then persuade your local paper to let you write a story about them, with a photo.

Information file

Voluntary work camps

Every summer, thousands of young people join in 'voluntary work camps' all over Britain (and in Europe). Just for the fun of it (without pay), they work together to do things like restore old railways, help run children's playschemes, make videos, restore country footpaths, and do archaeological digs. Food and accommodation is free, and the DHSS allows unemployed people to join in too. It makes for a great holiday, with a difference.

For information: (a) Write to International Voluntary Service, 53 Regent Street, Leicester LE1 6YL
(b) Write for a free copy of *Spare time, Share time*, from the National Youth Bureau, 17 Albion St, Leicester LE1 6GD. (Enclose large stamped addressed envelope)
(c) Write to the British Trust for Conservation Volunteers, 36 St Mary's St, Wallingford, Oxon. In Scotland, write for a copy of *Volunteering in Scotland*, from the Scottish Community Education Council, Atholl House, 2 Canning St, Edinburgh EH3 8EG

Community Service Volunteers (CSV)

CSV is a national organisation which involves young people in full-time voluntary work for up to a year. The work? Caring for others, and working for change in society. Looking after young children in nurseries and playgroups, joining in community arts groups or housing groups, working with physically or mentally handicapped people, teaching swimming to handicapped children. Anyone who applies to CSV is guaranteed a place somewhere in the country (away from home) within three months. You get free board and lodging, and weekly pocket money.

For full details, write to CSV, 237 Pentonville Road, London N1 9NJ.

Duke of Edinburgh's Award groups give you a chance to develop skills. Write for details to Duke of Edinburgh's Award, 5 Prince of Wales Terrace, London W8, or ask at the library for the local group.

Outward Bound courses offer adventurous training courses both in the wild and in the city. There are sometimes schemes to cover fees for unemployed people. Write to Outward Bound (City Challenge), Canal House, Drapers Field, Coventry CV1 4LG.

The Drake Fellowship offers a ten-day residential course for unemployed people aged 16–24 including transport for only £30, including five days out on exhibition. Once you have completed the basic course, there are a variety of Follow-On Projects, including sailing on a Cornish Shrimper (cost £1 per day). Write to The Drake Fellowship, 10 Trinity Square, London EC3P 3AX.

YMCA leadership courses are open to young unemployed people aged 17–23 who have shown willingness and aptitude in working for the good of their community. Courses last 14 days, and cost £20. Write to Leadership Co-ordinator, YMCA National Centre, Ulverston, Cumbria LA12 8BD.

Action Sport: In many cities, there are now active sports projects, and unemployed football leagues. In Wales, the Wales TUC organised a 'Dole Olympics' in 1985. In Leicester, there is a weekly programme of free sports activities all over the city. Contact the youth service, centre for the unemployed or council leisure services department.

Money: (1) If you want to do something active which will help you to develop your life, but you've got no money, The Prince's Trust may be able to help with a grant of up to £300. Write to Prince's Trust, Royal Jubilee Trusts, 8 Bedford Row, London WC1R 4BU.

One man's success – through active unemployment

Tommy Wilson's tale

Tommy Wilson's parents think he's daft. He had a steady job as an apprentice jeweller, but gave it up. The money was poor and he didn't like the work. But for a 19-year-old from the Gorbals in Glasgow, voluntary unemployment is enough to make his parents' blood boil. But that's Tommy.

Now he's living off £27 a week dole money and is technically unemployed. He's available for work, as they say. Then again, he's not exactly lying around the house. Six months into his new status, Tommy is a changed man. And it happened for a simple reason: he's got involved in the community.

That means, along with other things, he's trying to start a community business by setting up a recording studio in the Gorbals, he's behind GOODY (Gorbals Organisation on Development for Youth) and he's helping to set up an advice centre for young people in Glasgow. Then there's the couple of hours as a youth club leader with the unemployed workers centre. For good measure, there's Gorbals Promotions which puts on bands in the Gorbals, playing to audiences of 300 young people.

So Tommy does not hang around. He's up in the mornings and works well into the evening, planning, organising, going to meetings and getting things done. That's the motivation: trying to help young people in the Gorbals, and giving them a voice so that they can speak to the decision-makers themselves.

Tommy came into voluntary community work by accident. With his mate, Martin, the plan was to become overnight-millionaires, running a recording studio, putting on bands and being kings of the Glasgow music world. They made a good start as budding entrepreneurs, getting all the advice they could and even fixing up premises in the city centre – all without a penny to their name (Glasgow patter gets you a long way). That plan, though, has been revised over the past few months as they've talked to youth enquiry staff at the Adelphi Education Centre in the Gorbals. Now it's about setting up a local music centre for local bands as a community business.

'I realised that there was more to life than personal gain,' says Tommy, 'and that it should really be for the benefit of the community. It's really needed.'

Tommy admits he's come out of himself in the last six months, learning new skills – like speaking in public, basic administration, and organising – and getting a new outlook on life. He's met lots of local people, officials and anyone who can help young people in the Gorbals. 'I've also done more work in the last three months than in two years of working.'

(Courtesy of SCAN magazine)

- 'Tommy Wilson is stupid to do all that work when he could be sitting at home watching TV.'
  Agree ☐ Disagree ☐

- 'I admire what Tommy Wilson is doing, but I could never do all that myself.'
  Agree ☐ Disagree ☐

- 'I'd like to get involved in my own community in the same kind of way that Tommy Wilson has.'
  Agree ☐ Disagree ☐

Self-employment

Attitudes

(Scale of 0–5. 0 = Disagree strongly, 5 = Agree strongly)

- 'I would love to be able to earn my own living, quite soon, if someone would simply help me to get started.' 0 1 2 3 4 5
- 'This self-employment idea is just a big con, designed to create lots of badly paid jobs.'
  0 1 2 3 4 5
- 'I would like to earn my own living, but I haven't got the skills or the knowledge I would need.'
  0 1 2 3 4 5
- 'It's a waste of time working to earn a living, when you can get the dole for free.' 0 1 2 3 4 5

The arguments for self-employment

Give each argument a score from 0 to 10, depending on how strong each reason seems to be to you (10 for the strongest reasons).

☐ I would be getting experience and developing my confidence

☐ I would be learning how to organise myself and make plans

☐ I would be free and independent, with nobody telling me what to do

☐ I could work when I wanted, and stop work when I wanted

☐ There would be no limit on how much I could earn

☐ I would be free from signing on, and the hassles that go with it

☐ I could still look for jobs while I was working as self-employed

☐ It would help me at interviews and on job application forms

☐ It would be useful experience if I wanted to try it again later in life

☐ It could be fun, especially if I worked together with a friend

TOTAL (maximum 100)

The arguments against self-employment

Give each argument a score from 0 to 10, depending on how strong each reason seems to be to you (10 for the strongest reasons).

☐ I don't want to do that kind of work

☐ I haven't got enough confidence

☐ It wouldn't leave me enough time to do all the other things I want to do

☐ I am not good enough at organising myself

☐ I would not like working on my own

☐ I would rather get a guaranteed income each week from benefit

☐ I couldn't do car-washing or gardening in really cold or wet weather

☐ I wouldn't like the uncertainty of it

☐ I'd be no good at getting up in the morning unless I really had to

☐ It sounds too much like hard work

TOTAL (maximum 100)

What is your overall score?

Your score will help you to decide whether you think self-employment is right for you or not. You might of course score more (or less) tomorrow or next week, depending on how you felt. Read through page 42 as well, which will help you to think further about it.

☐ (A) Total score FOR self-employment

☐ (B) Total score AGAINST self-employment

The difference between the largest and the smallest is *THE RESULT*

= ☐ points FOR/AGAINST self-employment (maximum 100).

Which of the following real businesses do you think are run by young people under 24, in Britain?

☐ 1 Pet shop   ☐ 11 Sign-writer

☐ 2 Florist   ☐ 12 Shoemaker

☐ 3 Butcher   ☐ 13 Bicycle repairs

☐ 4 Computer software company   ☐ 14 Chemical factory

☐ 5 Shipping agents   ☐ 15 Oil exporter

☐ 6 Carpet importer   ☐ 16 Games publisher

☐ 7 Publisher   ☐ 17 Cabinet-maker

☐ 8 Design studio   ☐ 18 Glass-engraver

☐ 9 Dressmaker   ☐ 19 Taxi service

☐ 10 Photographer   ☐ 20 Builder

(For answers see page 47)

Action-learning

● Contact the nearest Local Enterprise Agency (or council economic development officer), and ask for information about young people who have set up their own businesses. Get in touch with them, and ask if they would let you interview them. Then ask them
(1) how they got started
(2) what their main difficulties have been
(3) what they think the most important factors are to succeed in business as a young person.

Then write a short series for a local paper or magazine about them, or produce a programme about them on local radio.

● Divide your group up, and write letters to the following organisations, asking them for information about the support which they can offer to young people starting up in business:
The Prince's Youth Business Initiative, 8 Bedford Row, London WC1R 4BU
'Livewire', 60 Grainger Street, Newcastle upon Tyne NE1 5JG
The Enterprise Allowance Scheme, c/o Jobcentres
The National Youth Bureau, 17 Albion Street, Leicester LE1 6GD
The nearest Local Enterprise Agency
The local Youth Service
The local council
The local Chamber of Commerce, and bank managers

Then have each person or group present what they have learnt to the rest of the group.

● Set up your own mini-company or mini-co-operative in your group, choosing something to make or some service to offer, and going through the whole process of running the business together. This takes several months, and it is an excellent way to learn what business involves. For proper details, write to Mini-Enterprise in Schools Project, Education Department, Warwick University, Westwood, Coventry CV4 7AL.

Brainstorm

You want to start up a business, and you have **baking skills**. Do a group brainstorm (see p 32) to discover as many ways as possible in which you might be able to earn a living from your baking.

Imagine . . .

Imagine that you are planning to start up a business making home-made pies to sell to local shops. Listed below are some of the steps that you might take. Number the steps in the order in which you might take them, from 1 to 7:

☐	● Finding premises where you can make the pies
☐	● Raising the money you need to get started
☐	● Attending a small business training course, or getting proper advice on how to start up a business
☐	● Doing market research to find out if there is a market for your pies
☐	● Practising making pies that people love to eat
☐	● Working out what your income and expenditure might look like for your first year in business
☐	● Starting to sell your pies among your friends, and on a street stall

(For answers see page 47)

Making your business succeed

What do you think are the important things which will make a young person's business succeed? Place the following factors in order, from 1 to 10, where 1 is most important:

☐	● Having a good product or service to offer
☐	● Being friendly and polite to customers
☐	● Doing proper market research beforehand
☐	● Putting effort into well-organised advertising and marketing
☐	● Working hard at your business
☐	● Learning how to do proper business and financial planning
☐	● Developing good intuition about possible business deals
☐	● Getting to love the process of being in business
☐	● Not trusting anyone, and keeping everything very secret
☐	● Being willing to ask for help when you get into difficulties

(For answers see page 47)

Further reading

Work for Yourself by Paddy Hall, (£2.50 from National Extension College, 18 Brooklands Avenue, Cambridge CB2 2HN); *Twenty Questions to Help You Choose a Business Idea* by David Grayson and David Irwin (£1 from Newcastle Youth Enterprise Centre, 45 Groat Market, Newcastle NE1 1UG); *Your Own Business* (£3.95 from Hobsons Publishing PLC, Bateman Street, Cambridge CB2 1LZ).

Your health

A B C

☐ ☐ ☐ How often do you get energetic exercise that makes you puff?
(a) Two or three times a week or more (b) Occasionally (c) Hardly ever

☐ ☐ ☐ 2 Do you smoke?
(a) Yes, 20 + a day (b) Yes, 2–19 a day (c) No

☐ ☐ ☐ 3 Do you have a sport that you enjoy whenever you can?
(a) Yes (b) Yes, but irregularly (c) No

☐ ☐ ☐ 4 Do you drink sweetened drinks (fizzy pop, etc)?
(a) Yes, every day (b) Yes, once or twice a week (c) No

☐ ☐ ☐ 5 Do you eat sweets, chocolates, etc?
(a) Yes, every day (b) Yes, once or twice a week (c) No

☐ ☐ ☐ 6 Do you eat fresh fruit or raw vegetables?
(a) Yes, every day (b) Yes, several days a week (c) Hardly ever

☐ ☐ ☐ 7 Do you eat frozen, tinned or instant food?
(a) Yes, all the time (b) Quite often (c) Hardly ever

☐ ☐ ☐ 8 Do you do daily stretch, aerobic and/or breathing exercises?
(a) Yes, every day (b) Sometimes (c) No, never

☐ ☐ ☐ 9 Do you drink alcohol?
(a) Less than one pint or short a week (b) Several pints or shorts a week (c) A pint or short or more every day

☐ ☐ ☐ 10 Do you feel fit?
(a) Yes, all the time
(b) Sometimes (c) Not really

☐ ☐ ☐ 11 Do you often get colds, backaches, headaches, stomach cramps or other ills and pains?
(a) Hardly ever (b) Yes, occasionally (c) Yes, quite often

☐ ☐ ☐ 12 Do you enjoy being inside your own body?
(a) No, not really (b) Yes, most of the time (c) Yes, all the time

☐ ☐ ☐ 13 Do you do meditation, deep breathing or any other relaxation exercise?
(a) Yes, regularly (b) Sometimes (c) No

☐ ☐ ☐ 14 How often do you get out into the fresh open air, and get it into your lungs by walking or cycling around?
(a) Only when I'm dragged out (b) Sometimes (c) As often as I can

☐ ☐ ☐ 15 How many press-ups can you do **right now**? (test yourself)
(a) Less than 5 (b) 6–14 (c) 15+

☐ ☐ ☐ 16 How far could you run right now, without stopping?
(a) Four miles or more
(b) ½–4 miles (c) Less than ½ mile

☐ ☐ ☐ 17 Do you ever eat 100% brown bread?
(a) Yes, very often (b) Sometimes (c) Not if I can avoid it

☐ ☐ ☐ 18 Do you easily share your feelings with close friends?
(a) No, I find it very difficult (b) Sometimes (c) Yes, often

☐ ☐ ☐ 19 Do you spend much time worrying, or preoccupied with depressing thoughts?
(a) Yes (b) Yes, sometimes (c) No – I have mostly happy, positive thoughts

☐ ☐ ☐ 20 (Invent your own question)

Scoring: After discussion, choose the scores for each question which you think are appropriate. Then find your scores for each other. Alternatively, use the scoring below, which is very simple, and intended to stimulate you to create your own scoring system.

Questions 1, 3, 6, 8, 9, 10, 11, 13, 16, 17: (a) 2, (b) 1, (c) 0
Questions 2, 4, 5, 7, 12, 14, 15, 18, 19: (a) 0, (b) 1, (c) 2.

Score: 30–40 You're in pretty good shape!
20–29 You're not doing so bad, but you'd feel healthier if you took more exercise and/or ate healthier food.
10–19 Look at it this way – you've got plenty of room for improvement.
0– 9 You've got even **more** room for improvement!

- 'The mind is very powerful – having negative thoughts can make you ill, and having positive thoughts can keep you well.'
Agree/disagree/not sure
- 'Things like meditation and yoga can make a huge difference to a person's life, by helping them to develop inner stillness.'
Agree/disagree/not sure
- 'Life is simply a material process. There is no such thing as "spirit" or "soul".'
Agree/disagree/not sure
- 'We haven't really begun to understand the human mind, the brain, or the secrets of life yet.'
Agree/disagree/not sure
- 'The education system ought to teach us how to develop as complete human beings, and let us explore our full potential, emotionally, spiritually and psychically, as well as physically and mentally.'
Agree/disagree/not sure

Your relationships

Unhappy relationships with our close friends, our families and our partners can undermine all our efforts to reach our goals.

Agree ☐ Disagree ☐ Not sure ☐

If we feel emotionally hurt, angry, rejected, misunderstood or unhappy, everything else begins to seem much more difficult.

Agree ☐ Disagree ☐ Not sure ☐

There are no easy answers to emotional problems, but recognising them and being willing to talk about them is an important first step.

Agree ☐ Disagree ☐ Not sure ☐

(Note for tutor: it is suggested that while this questionnaire can be used in a group, and can lead to valuable group discussion, it is only proper to let people keep privacy on any of their answers if they wish to.)

1 How happy are you about your relationship with your mother (or stepmother)? (0 = Very unhappy, 10 = Very happy)
0 1 2 3 4 5 6 7 8 9 10

2 How happy are you about your relationship with your father (or stepfather)?
0 1 2 3 4 5 6 7 8 9 10

3 How happy are you about your relationship with . . . (a brother, sister or close friend)?
0 1 2 3 4 5 6 7 8 9 10

4 How easy or difficult do you find it to talk about your close personal feelings? (0 = Very easy, 10 = Very difficult)
0 1 2 3 4 5 6 7 8 9 10

5 How often did you talk about your feelings in the family in which you grew up? (0 = Never at all, 10 = Very often)
0 1 2 3 4 5 6 7 8 9 10

6 When you get upset by something, what do you usually do?

☐ Get angry

☐ Sulk, and get moody

☐ Feel hurt, and maybe cry

☐ Laugh, pretend it hasn't happened

☐ Withdraw into myself, and hide my feelings

☐ Let people know my feelings, in a clear way

☐ Write about it – a poem, a song, a letter

☐ Find someone to talk with about it

☐ Feel upset for a while, and then forget it

7 How happy are you with touching people, and with being touched? (0 = Not at all happy, 10 = Completely happy)
0 1 2 3 4 5 6 7 8 9 10

8 How do you usually solve or react to arguments and quarrels?

☐ By exploding into a rage

☐ By shouting

☐ By arguing, and trying to win

☐ By trying to manipulate the other person

☐ By trying to please the other person

☐ By crying

☐ By going silent, and refusing to talk about it

☐ By sitting down together to talk it through

☐ By finding a third person to help us sort it out

☐ By just letting it drop

9 How easy or difficult do you find it to start up personal love-relationships? (boyfriend, girlfriend, partner, etc) (0 = Very easy, 10 = Very difficult)
0 1 2 3 4 5 6 7 8 9 10

10 How easy or difficult do you find it to keep a good love-relationship going, once it has started? (0 = Very easy, 10 = Very difficult)
0 1 2 3 4 5 6 7 8 9 10

11 Most people have difficulties in the process of building a good relationship. What do you find to be your own biggest difficulties in your personal love-relationships? Give each item a score from 0 to 10 (0 = Not a difficulty at all, 10 = A very big difficulty).

- [ ] Not being able to talk together easily
- [ ] Not being able to share our feelings together easily
- [ ] Feeling irritation, anger or hostility at each other
- [ ] Getting into arguments and fights together
- [ ] Not listening to each other
- [ ] One partner dominating the other
- [ ] Our sex life
- [ ] Lack of privacy together
- [ ] Not feeling confident enough in myself, and sometimes feeling threatened by my partner
- [ ] Jealousy
- [ ] Fear that my partner will leave me
- [ ] Physical violence
- [ ] Shopping expeditions
- [ ] My partner's family and parents
- [ ] Coping with our child or children
- [ ] Unemployment, lack of money and hope in the future
- [ ] Feeling that my partner is interfering in my life
- [ ] Fears that I may have chosen the wrong partner

12 Can you talk about the following with the people listed below? (Either simply tick, or give each a score from 0 to 10, where 0 = Never, 10 = Very often.)

	Mother	Father	Girl/boy friend	Best friend	Workmates schoolmates
Personal feelings					
Worries					
Family problems					
World affairs					
Sex					
Spiritual/ religious matters					
Your own personal interests					
Your dreams, your hopes					

13 How important do you think it is for a person to be able to give and receive love? (0 = Not important at all, 10 = Very important)

0 1 2 3 4 5 6 7 8 9 10

14 How difficult or easy do *you* find it to give and receive love? (0 = Very easy, 10 = Very difficult)

0 1 2 3 4 5 6 7 8 9 10

15 How difficult or easy do you find it to be honest in questionnaires like these? (0 = Very easy, 10 = Very difficult)
(a) Assuming that your answers will be totally private

0 1 2 3 4 5 6 7 8 9 10

(b) Assuming that you may be asked to share your answers in the group

0 1 2 3 4 5 6 7 8 9 10

The meaning of life

Ask yourself the following questions:

1 When you look at a butterfly, a new-born child or a beautiful flower, do you **feel** that life has meaning? Yes/no

2 When you look at a dirty city street, and concrete tower blocks, do you feel that life has meaning? Yes/no

3 When you think about the nuclear missiles, and the destruction of the Amazonian rainforest, and the terrible things that people do to each other in time of war, do you think that life has any meaning? Yes/no

4 When you think of someone whom you love, or of some place that you love, or of the things that you long for in life, do you think that life has meaning? Yes/no

5 Do you think that you understand what life is all about? Yes/no/I'm working on it

6 Why do you think that people created the world's religions?

☐ To take away the fear of death

☐ To create comfort, against the reality of sorrow and pain

☐ To keep people from asking their own questions about life

☐ To convey hidden truths and wisdoms and mysteries about life to other people

☐ Because they totally believed that some great religious teacher spoke the truth (eg Christ, Buddha, Mohammed or _____)

☐ To persuade people to act with love and compassion, and not to behave in cruel, bad (or 'evil') ways

☐ I haven't a clue

☐

7 How often do you have times when you feel really awful, sad, and empty, and when you wonder why people bother to live? (0 = Never, 10 = Very often)
    0 1 2 3 4 5 6 7 8 9 10

8 How often do you have times when you feel truly wonderful, excited, and really glad to be alive? (0 = Never, 10 = Very often)
    0 1 2 3 4 5 6 7 8 9 10

9 What do you think might happen when we die?

☐ We just cease existing altogether – the end

☐ We become ghosts

☐ We go either to heaven or to hell

☐ We may wait for a while, and then we reincarnate as a new human child

☐ We may wait for a while, and then we reincarnate as a human, or as an animal or insect

☐ We leave our bodies, and float around, until we finally travel off to another realm

☐ We become absorbed into the spiritual essence of all things

☐ I really don't know

10 Which of the following do you think may encourage people to feel that there may be meaning in life?

☐ Finding out about ancient mysteries or the possible existence of other beings in the universe

☐ Belonging to a religion or religious group

☐ Really enjoying life

☐ Going through really hard times, and discovering a sense of inner purpose

☐ Having lots of money

☐ Learning meditation, or contemplation

☐ Discovering what kind of work you really want to do in life, and being able to do it

☐ Knowing that you are loved by other people

☐ Loving yourself

☐ Living in a beautiful area

☐ Living or working co-operatively with other people, and enjoying good friendship, lots of laughter, and good personal support

☐ Working for a 'cause' or a purpose, such as working with young handicapped children, campaigning to create jobs locally, saving the Amazonian rain-forest, or trying to end famine in the world

☐ Spending time reading and thinking about life, and continually asking questions

11 (a) Try to describe what 'infinity' is.
   (b) Try to describe what 'the edge of space' might be like.
   (c) Try to describe what the 'end of time' might be like.

12 Who do you think might really begin to understand what life is all about?

☐ The American President

☐ The Pope

☐ The astronauts and cosmonauts

☐ People who have experienced great suffering

☐ Some scientists

☐ One of your parents, or grandparents

- [ ] Indian gurus and yogis
- [ ] Healers, shamans and magicians
- [ ] Animals, trees
- [ ] People from other planets
- [ ] Great philosophers
- [ ] The people who set school exams
- [ ] People who have died
- [ ] Nobody at all

13 Do you need to understand what life is all about in order to feel that it has meaning? Yes/no

14 Do you need to feel hopeful about life, in order to feel that life has meaning? Yes/no

15 If you were with a personal friend who was depressed and fed up, and who felt that life had no meaning, what do you think would be the most helpful thing to do?

- [ ] Give him/her a warm hug
- [ ] Spend some time together, being friendly and supportive
- [ ] Encourage him/her to talk about his/her worries and feelings
- [ ] Encourage him/her to have a holiday, and to get away for a few days
- [ ] Encourage him/her to go and talk to somebody whom he/she respect and trusts
- [ ] Go and ask for advice from someone whom **you** trust, to ask for suggestions about what you could do

- [ ] I don't know
- [ ] _____

16 Do you believe that humans will one day discover what life is all about, what happens on the other side of the universe, and what happens after death?
Yes [ ] No [ ] Maybe [ ]

17 Do you believe that there is more to life than simply material existence?
Yes [ ] No [ ]

18 Create your own question, to ask the others in your group, about the meaning of life: _____

Action-learning

Break up into pairs, and go out into the streets with these three questions. Be prepared to stay with each person for up to 15 minutes, if necessary, as they are not easy questions to answer, and to write down their words when they reply, to bring back to the group.

A Do you think that life has any meaning?

B If 'no', can you think of anything that you would like to change, that might give life meaning?

C If 'yes', can you say what it is in life that gives it meaning, for you?

Further reading: *The New Unemployment Handbook* by Guy Dauncey and Jane Mountain (National Extension College 1987, 18 Brooklands Ave, Cambridge CB2 2HN, £4.50)
Nice Work If You Can Get It by Guy Dauncey, National Extension College 1983 (£2.50)

Answers to quizzes, etc

Page 22: 1 – True. 2 – False. There were 350,000 trainees in 1986. 3 – False. 4 – False. You should get at least 1½ days holiday for every month you work on YTS. 5 – True. 6 – True. 7 – False. YTS is a training scheme for young adults, and is not like school at all. 8 – True. 9 – True. Most learning on YTS is by learning by experience, and not from books or blackboards. 10 – False. The pay in 1986 was £27.30 in the first year and £35 in the second year. 11 – True. 'Project Genesis' is a special YTS business programme. 12 – True. 13 – False. 14 – False. 15 – False. 16 – True. 17 – False. You may learn these skills while on YTS, but they are not part of the 'core skills' taught on every scheme. 18 – True. 19 – True. Trainees on a YTS scheme in Kent have developed their own falconry, after seeing the film 'Kes'. 20 – True. 'Personal Effectiveness' training helps you to enjoy better interpersonal relationships – which ought to mean that you also enjoy a happier love life.

Page 26: Qu 3 – all except banking; Qu 6 – the Jobcentre and the college.

Page 28: A mixture of different factors.

Page 36: All are 'yes', except 5 and 16.

Page 41: All except nos 14 and 15 are real.

Page 42: Possible solution to 'Imagine': 5, 7, 3, 4, 6, 2, 1
'Making Your Business Succeed': There is no one correct solution. The correct order will differ for every young person.

Training, unemployment... and the meaning of life helps you to explore and understand more about your own life, your future, your dreams, and how you can make plans to realise your hopes.

● It is packed full of exercises and action-learning suggestions on almost every page.

Contents

Introduction	2	Working and learning	21
How do you see yourself?	4	Your choices – YTS True or False	22
How do you view life in general?	5	YTS Questionnaire	23
What do you hope for in life?	11	YTS Action-learning	24
What are your dreams?	12	The Community Programme	25
What is 'success'?	13	Full-time training and education	26
Who supports/discourages you?	15	Active unemployment	27
What kind of supports do you have?	16	Self-employment	41
What stops you?	17	Your health	43
Your personal power	18	Your relationships	44
Personal goals and strategies	19	The meaning of life	46

The author

Guy Dauncey is a freelance writer, organiser and trainer who has spent many years working in and around the issues of unemployment, personal and community development, and positive approaches to life. He divides his time between London and Winnipeg, Canada. He is a member of the Green Party, and a friend of the Findhorn Foundation in Scotland. Among his other books are *The New Unemployment Handbook* and *Nice Work If You Can Get It* (National Extension College, Cambridge).

The CRAC Survival and Job Skills series

My Job Application Book
Claims, Benefits, YTS and Your Rights
Your First Move
Your Own Business
Into Work and Training
Write Your Own CV
Coping as a Young Adult
Improve Your Study Skills
Is It A Fair Deal?

Published by Hobsons Publishing PLC, Bateman Street, Cambridge CB2 1LZ

> *People think that all black girls want to do is have kids, get a flat and live off Social Security. But I don't. I want to be independent. I don't want even to live off any man. I don't want that, I want to be one of those independent women, so like if I do have kids, I know that I could bring them up, if he's not around. That's the sort of life I want. I'm determined to get it, but determination's not everything.*
>
> *I believe in myself. It's a good thing, really, if you believe in yourself, cos it keeps you upright. It's when you stop believing in yourself, that you start going down.*

Sharon

ISBN 0-86021-934-8